Wisdom for Life

DEVOTIONAL

GAIL BURTON PURATH

Wisdom for Life

DEVOTIONAL

100 **One-Minute** Reflections from

Psalms & Proverbs

B&H
PUBLISHING
BRENTWOOD, TENNESSEE

Published by B&H Publishing Group
Brentwood, Tennessee

Dewey Decimal Classification: 242.5
Subject Heading: DEVOTIONAL LITERATURE / CHRISTIAN LIFE / BIBLE. O.T.
PSALMS / BIBLE. O.T. PROVERBS

Cover design by B&H Publishing Group. Cover photo by Kelly Knox/Stocksy.
Author photo by Patton Portraits Photography.

1 2 3 4 5 6 · 26 25 24 23

I dedicate this book to my husband and best friend, Michael, who shares my love for the Lord. He has been a constant source of love, encouragement, and wisdom.

Acknowledgments

I'm so grateful for the challenges, hardships, and sorrows God has allowed in my life. That may sound like a strange way to start the acknowledgments for a book, but hardships have molded my faith in powerful ways (Rom. 8:28). Without them, I'd never have known how God comforts the brokenhearted (Ps. 147:3; 2 Cor. 1:3-4). I'd never have realized that in His strength I can do things I could never do in my own strength (Phil. 4:13). I'd never have grown in perseverance and trust (Rom. 5:1-5).

Through hardships I came to understand how important God's Word is to the well-being of my soul (Ps. 18:30). That led me to start my devotional blog Bible Love Notes, and eventually led to the publishing of *Wisdom for Life*. So, I thank the Lord for teaching me things through my hardships that I could never have learned otherwise.

I also thank my faithful Bible Love Notes readers who've challenged me with their questions, blessed me with their faith stories, and encouraged me to write a book of my devotions. I thank my terrific staff of volunteer translators, who've expanded the ministry to other nations and blessed me with their godly hearts. And I give a special thanks to Cathy Libby, a lifetime missionary in Suriname, who volunteered to edit my online devotions and ended up becoming one of my dearest friends. All of these people and situations have helped me improve my writing skills, preparing me to write this book.

I also thank my faithful friends who've encouraged me and prayed for me and spurred me on to love and good works (Heb. 10:24). And my best friend and husband, Michael, deserves special thanks. I could not have completed this manuscript were it not for his daily help and encouragement. He's been God's gift to me for more than fifty years, and a daily reminder of God's love, forgiveness, and faithfulness.

Last but not least, I thank my agent Dan Balow for encouraging me to publish a book and B&H Publishing Group for giving me that opportunity. May God's purposes be fully served in the publishing of *Wisdom for Life*!

Introduction

As a deer longs for flowing streams, so I long for you, God.

(Psalm 42:1)

Wisdom for Life is designed to give you a deeper appreciation for the books of Psalms and Proverbs. These Old Testament wisdom books bring us peace, give us comfort, guide our decisions, correct our misunderstandings, and teach us truths that help us mature in our faith. Whether you're a new student of the Bible or a mature believer, *Wisdom for Life* offers relevant insights for your daily life.

The devotions take only one minute to read, making them easy to fit into a busy schedule. But they offer multiple Scripture references and a "For Further Thought" section so you can dig deeper when you have the time.

The first few devotions are mini Bible lessons that will help you better understand the unique purposes God has built into Psalms and Proverbs. They are designed to lay the foundation for the rest of the book.

Although *Wisdom for Life* is designed for individual devotional use, it easily lends itself to family devotions or small-group study. See the appendix for ideas and suggestions.

My prayer is that each devotion will draw you closer to the Lord.

> But as for me, it is good for me to draw near to
>   God;
> I have made the Lord GOD my refuge *and* placed
>   my trust in Him,
> That I may tell of all Your works.
> (Ps. 73:28 AMP)

A Woman of the Word

Isn't it wonderful that the Creator of the universe cares so deeply about our lives that He gave us a book to help us through our time on earth and prepare us for our life in eternity? When we realize our need for God's Word, it's life changing. We begin to see the power and understanding Scripture gives us, the wisdom and truth it provides, and the nourishment it offers our hearts, souls, and minds.

We can say with the psalmist: "I rejoice in the way revealed by your decrees as much as in all riches. I will meditate on your precepts and think about your ways. I will delight in your statutes; I will not forget your word" (Ps. 119:14–16).

God reveals Himself in His written Word. May it be our most valuable resource as we seek to know Him intimately. Let me share a poem I wrote that communicates my prayer for you, for myself, and for all Christ followers.

A Woman of the Word

By Gail Burton Purath

The Bible wore her imprint
It's cover soft from use
The pages rubbed and wrinkled
The binding coming loose

And even if this Christian
And her Bible were apart
She still would have it with her
Hidden in her heart

Oh, make me such a woman, Lord
Who hungers to be fed
Who cherishes a line from You
More than her daily bread

And when my days are over
May it be my epitaph
"She longed to spend
More time with Him
And now is doing that."

For Further Thought

As you begin this devotional book, would you pray that it increases your love and respect for God and gives you a deepening desire to spend time in His Word?

Prophecy, Principles, Praise, and Problem-Solving

How relevant is the book of Psalms for modern Christians? Is it simply an archaic book of poetry, prayers, and songs? Nothing could be further from the truth. The book of Psalms is significant in a number of ways:

1. *Prophecy*. It contains important predictions of future events. For example, Psalm 22:1 predicts Christ's exact words from the cross (Matt. 27:46).

2. *Principles*. It reinforces biblical truths. In the New Testament, Psalms is one of the most quoted of the Old Testament books. Just a few examples: Jesus quotes Psalm 110:1 to explain that He is both God and man, son of David and son of God (Luke 20:41–44). In Acts 4:25–26, the believers quote Psalm 2:1–2 and explain that God's Holy Spirit was speaking through David when he wrote the psalm.

3. *Praise*. It teaches us how to exalt the Lord. The prayers and poetry of the psalms reveal the glory of our Lord and remind us that everything that has breath should be praising Him (Ps. 150).

4. *Problem-solving.* It teaches us how to deal with our problems biblically. The psalmists shared their sorrow, confusion, and trials with the Lord, and with His help they lived victoriously. Their conversations with God teach us that we can also take our problems to the Lord because "God is our refuge and strength, a helper who is always found in times of trouble" (Ps. 46:1).

Not only does Psalms offer prophecy, principles, praise, and problem-solving, it's also beautifully poetic.

For Further Thought

Do you have a favorite psalm? If so, why is it your favorite? Does it contain prophecy, principles, praise, problem-solving, or a combination?

Old Letters in the Attic

Do you have a "memory box" filled with old letters that have special meaning to you? I do. I have some letters my father wrote when I was in grade school and he was working overseas. They reveal so much about his personality and his love for me, my mom, and my sisters. I also have some childhood letters from my grandmother that contain wonderful examples of her faith in Christ and her fun personality.

Imagine finding such a box in your grandmother's attic filled with letters sent to your great-grandfather from his children. As you read the letters, you discover that this family patriarch was a loving and wise man whose children often asked him for help. Their written words reveal a deep respect for his character and a strong dependence on his guidance.

In some ways, this describes the Psalms because they were written by God's children, asking Him hard questions, seeking His help and comfort, and praising His faithfulness and character. Of course, the book of Psalms is also divinely inspired. Like the rest of God's Word, it is "God-breathed," given to us by God Himself to bring light and understanding into our lives (2 Tim. 3:16 NIV; Ps. 119:130).

When we study the letters, songs, and poems in Psalms, we grow in our understanding of God's character. We see Him through the eyes of His children who pleased Him, disappointed Him, suffered for Him, shared His glory, and asked Him difficult questions. It's like finding a wonderful box of old letters, only better.

For Further Thought

Perhaps you can easily understand this analogy because you have a family member whom you seek for godly counsel. Or perhaps you've never had that blessing. But every believer can have this relationship with God. Why not write a letter to Him today, sharing your concerns, questions, and appreciation?

The Relevance of the Psalms

I'm always amazed at how relevant the psalms are when we're struggling through difficulties.

Has someone slandered you? The psalmist knew this injustice: "All who hate me whisper together about me; they plan to harm me" (Ps. 41:7).

Have you shown kindness to someone who later turned on you? The psalmist felt this pain: "They repay me evil for good, and hatred for my love" (Ps. 109:5).

Have you loved someone sacrificially only to have them reject you? The psalmist grieved this situation: "Even my friend in whom I trusted, one who ate my bread, has raised his heel against me" (Ps. 41:9).

Are you confused by the way evil men triumph? This question confused many of the psalmists: "Look at them—the wicked! They are always at ease, and they increase their wealth. Did I purify my heart and wash my hands in innocence for nothing?" (Ps. 73:12–13).

Sometimes when reading a psalm, I pause and breathe a sigh, realizing I'm not alone. Others have felt the same way I'm feeling. And they took their feelings to their best Friend, the Lord. It's such a blessing to know that God isn't offended by our honest questions and raw feelings. And it's important to know that others have faced similar problems and found comfort and help in the Lord (Heb. 12:1–2).

Like the psalmist I can say, "I called to the LORD in my distress, and I cried to my God for help. From his temple he heard my voice, and my cry to him reached his ears" (Ps. 18:6).

For Further Thought

According to the combined messages of Psalm 34:17–19; James 1:2–4; and 1 Peter 4:12–19, in what ways does God rescue us from all our troubles?

Figurative and Poetic Language

Believing the Bible is the inerrant Word of God doesn't mean taking every word literally. Every word of God is true. We know that the stories and narratives in Scripture are historical facts. Jonah was swallowed by a big fish, and God parted the Red Sea. But we also recognize figurative language. God uses symbols, hyperbole, personification, metaphors, and other figurative prose to convey His message. This is often true in the poetic books like Psalms and Proverbs.

If we insist that every word of Scripture is literal, we'll have to deny satellite photography and claim that the earth is flat because Psalm 104:5 says, "He established the earth on its foundations; it will never be shaken." We'd also have to believe that rivers have literal hands and mountains have voices because Psalm 98:8 says, "Let the rivers clap their hands; let the mountains shout together for joy." We'd have to believe that wisdom is a woman who stands at the gate of the city because Proverbs 8 describes wisdom that way. We'd need to ask our doctors for a prescription of "joyful heart" because Proverbs 17:22 says: "A joyful heart is good medicine."

Recognizing figurative language in Scripture helps us avoid confusion and misunderstandings. And it's not hard to recognize because we use it frequently in our own conversations.

For Further Thought

Do you have a favorite figure of speech from Psalms and Proverbs? Examples from Proverbs:

- *Simile:* "A beautiful woman who rejects good sense is like a gold ring in a pig's snout" (Prov. 11:22).
- *Metaphor:* "A wise person's instruction is a fountain of life, turning people away from the snares of death" (Prov. 13:14).
- *Personification:* "Doesn't wisdom call out? Doesn't understanding make her voice heard? At the heights overlooking the road, at the crossroads, she takes her stand" (Prov. 8:1–2).

A Proverb a Day Keeps Stupidity Away

Many years ago when we lived in Germany, a soldier put a stocking cap over his face and robbed a bank. But he was immediately apprehended because he was wearing his uniform with his name tag clearly visible.

I'm glad when criminals lack common sense, but I hate it when I do something foolish. And God also wants us to avoid foolishness. That's one reason He gave us the book of Proverbs—general principles for doing what's right and avoiding foolishness.

> For gaining wisdom and instruction; . . . understanding words of insight; . . . receiving instruction in prudent behavior, doing what is right and just and fair, . . . giving prudence to those who are simple, knowledge and discretion to the young—let the wise listen and add to their learning, and let the discerning get guidance—for understanding proverbs and parables, the sayings and riddles of the wise. (Prov. 1:1–6 NIV)

Proverbs are not guarantees, but they are wonderful, practical, helpful guidelines. And Proverbs can be easily divided for study: It has thirty-one chapters, which means we can read one chapter each day and go through the entire book every month. Why not start the habit of "a chapter of Proverbs a day"?

For Further Thought

Using today's date, choose the chapter in Proverbs. Read through it and write down the verses that give you wisdom for your current situations. And remember, "A discerning mind seeks knowledge" (Prov. 15:14).

The Difference between a Proverb and a Promise

Proverbs 10:27 says, "The fear of the LORD prolongs life, but the years of the wicked are cut short." Does this mean we can determine a man's godliness by the length of his life? No. Godly lifestyles are better for our health and well-being, but some godly people die young, and some evil people live long lives.

Proverbs 10:4 says, "Idle hands make one poor, but diligent hands bring riches." Does this mean anyone who works hard will become rich? No. Laziness negatively affects our lives, but wealth and poverty are dependent on multiple factors.

Proverbs 16:7 says, "When a person's ways please the LORD, he makes even his enemies to be at peace with him." Does this mean anyone with enemies has displeased the Lord? No. Ungodly people tend to have more enemies, but godly people also have enemies. In fact, Jesus said, "You will be hated by everyone because of my name" (Matt. 10:22).

Proverbs is the divinely inspired Word of God, and its divinely inspired purpose is explained in Proverbs 1:1–6. It helps us gain wisdom and discipline by "understanding a proverb or a parable, the words of the wise, and their riddles" (v. 6). It's a book of concise biblical principles. It's not a book of promises. When we follow the instructions in Proverbs, we live wisely and biblically, but God doesn't guarantee that we'll always experience the desired results. In fact, Christ tells us to expect troubles in this world (John 16:33).

So let's be careful to correctly handle God's Word and realize that if a proverb is a promise, it will be confirmed as such in the New Testament (2 Tim. 2:15).

For Further Thought

Read through Proverbs 11 and list the verses that contain promises confirmed in the New Testament and the verses that are wise sayings, not promises.

The Beginning of Wisdom

The theme for the book of Proverbs is found in chapter 9 verse 10: "The fear of the LORD is the beginning of wisdom, and the knowledge of the Holy One is understanding."

Holy fear is best described as "reverence," but it's a powerful type of reverence. It's not "God is a good God." It's "Wow! God is awesome and glorious, able to create and destroy with a breath, Creator and Judge of all, all-powerful, all-knowing, all-wise. He defines and personifies love and truth."

People can have academic degrees and awards and still be little more than fools if they don't fear God. But God's true children trust Him when things go wrong. They seek Him when making decisions. They acknowledge that He is the ultimate source of truth. They won't accept any teaching that contradicts His Word.

God confides in God-fearers, giving them an understanding of things others cannot comprehend: "The secret counsel of the LORD is for those who fear him, and he reveals his covenant to them" (Ps. 25:14).

Do you fear Him?

For Further Thought

For a better understanding of what it means to fear the Lord, look through the passages below and note what characteristics and benefits they present:

> Who is this person who fears the LORD?
> He will show him the way he should choose.
> (Ps. 25:12)

> How great is your goodness,
> which you have stored up for those who fear you.
> In the presence of everyone you have acted
> for those who take refuge in you. (Ps. 31:19)

> But look, the LORD keeps his eye on those who
>   fear him—
> those who depend on his faithful love. (Ps. 33:18)

> God, you have heard my vows;
> you have given a heritage
> to those who fear your name. (Ps. 61:5)

> For as high as the heavens are above the earth,
> so great is his faithful love
> toward those who fear him. (Ps. 103:11)

> How happy is everyone who fears the LORD,
> who walks in his ways! (Ps. 128:1)

Good Prayers from Psalms

Praying Scripture offers benefits if we do it thoughtfully and deliberately. Speaking God's words can make our prayers more purposeful, and the book of Psalms contains some wonderful prayers to pray for this purpose.

For example, when we want to stay focused during our quiet time, we might pray Psalm 25:4–5: "Make your ways known to me, LORD; teach me your paths. Guide me in your truth and teach me, for you are the God of my salvation; I wait for you all day long."

If we want to make sure our thoughts and conversations please the Lord, we can pray Psalm 19:14: "May the words of my mouth and the meditation of my heart be acceptable to you, LORD, my rock and my Redeemer."

If we're feeling down and want to remind ourselves of God's faithfulness, we can pray Psalm 42:11: "Why, my soul, are you so dejected? Why are you in such turmoil? Put your hope in God, for I will still praise him, my Savior and my God."

If we're making a decision, we can pray Psalm 86:11: "Teach me your way, LORD, that I may rely on your faithfulness; give me an undivided heart, that I may fear your name" (NIV).

This is just a sampling of the many prayers Psalms provides, so pull out your Bible in your favorite translation and incorporate the Word of God in your prayers. You might even memorize prayers that are especially meaningful to you.

For Further Thought

God listens to our hearts. We don't need to say special words in order to get His attention. However, Isaiah 55:10–11 and Hebrews 4:12 explain some qualities of God's Word that give us reason to pray Scripture.

Facts, Wisdom, Knowledge, and Understanding

Genuine faith is built on reverence and trust in the Lord and His Word because "the fear of the LORD is the beginning of wisdom, and the knowledge of the Holy One is understanding" (Prov. 9:10). We learn who God is by reading His Word, and we discern truth from error by judging all things with God's Word.

It rarely happens overnight. Instead, it's a process of renewing our minds (Rom. 12:1-2). For example, a Christian may believe God used evolution to create the world until he discovers that the whole gospel is founded on the truth that sin brought death into God's perfect world and that sin was committed by fully formed human beings.

"The heavens were made by the word of the LORD, and all the stars, by the breath of his mouth" (Ps. 33:6). Why would God choose to speak millions of years of mutations, mistakes, and death into existence when He could create perfection with a word?

This is one of the many areas where we need to renew our minds in God's Word so we will "understand righteousness, justice, and integrity—every good path" (Prov. 2:9). Then wisdom will enter our hearts, and knowledge will delight us. Discretions will watch over us, and understanding will guard us (Prov. 2:9–11).

God's wisdom is essential for our spiritual well-being and essential for dividing truth from error. It helps us make wise decisions and avoid ungodly paths. It helps us reject things that appeal to our fallen human nature and embrace things that validate God's truth.

For Further Thought

Note how Proverbs 6:23; Psalm 18:30; and Psalm 12:6 confirm the truth of this devotion.

If you'd like to study the contradiction between evolution and creation, God's Word is ready to renew your mind: Genesis 1:29–31 explains that God's creation was very good. Romans 5:12 and 8:10 confirm that death was a result of sin. Romans 8:18–25 and Genesis 3:17–19 talk about sin's curse on the earth. Romans 1:20 tells us that creation is a reflection of God's divine nature and character, and 2 Peter 3:1–7 predicts that belief in creation will be a major stumbling block for mankind.

A Selfish Friend

Imagine you have a friend who's always asking you for help. She respects you, but the conversations always focus on her. You are constantly advising her and cheering her up, but she rarely acts grateful. I've had a few friends like that, and it's difficult. But I have to admit that I'm often selfish with my dearest Friend.

He's always available and, oh, so wise. When I call, His phone is never busy, He's never distracted, and He never puts me on hold. He knows me better than any human being and knows what I need before I even ask (Ps. 139:1–4).

Reading Psalm 119:164 made me realize how often I'm like a selfish friend when it comes to my Lord. In this verse, the psalmist says, "I praise you seven times a day for your righteous judgments." The author of this psalm loved God and His Word so much that he made a practice of praising the Lord seven times each day. He even got up at midnight for that purpose (Ps. 119:62).

When I compare this to my times of praise, I realize how often I take the Lord for granted and how seldom I make serious attempts to praise Him. In our house we usually set an alarm to go off every hour so we can stop and say a quick prayer, keeping focused on the Lord throughout the day. I typically make requests. But the psalmist's example encourages me to spend more time simply praising God.

Are you spending some time each day praising Him?

For Further Thought

Do you know which book of the Bible uses the word *praise* ten times more often than any other book? Hint: It contains the longest and shortest chapters in the Bible as well as the middle chapter of the Bible. Why not make your own "concordance" by keeping a journal of the passages in Scripture that contain the word *praise*?

Finding Strength in the Psalms

One morning when I was stressed and discouraged, I picked up my Bible and opened it to the book of Psalms. I knew that I needed God's Word to help me process my problems. And when I read Psalm 105:4, it stated the obvious truth I needed to hear that day: "Seek the LORD and his strength; seek his face always."

How many times had I read that simple command and others like it without fully comprehending the meaning? When I'm struggling, it's always because I'm trying to deal with things in my strength, not His. Self-help is a popular concept, but as Christians we know that our real strength comes from God, not from within ourselves.

Scripture repeatedly assures us that "God is our refuge and strength, a helper who is always found in times of trouble" (Ps. 46:1). He is "near all who call out to him, all who call out to him with integrity" (Ps. 145:18).

But how do we "call out to him with integrity"?

We acknowledge our need, admitting we can't do it on our own. We admit that we need His strength even when we aren't facing difficulties. And we realize that we find His strength through Scripture, prayer, and godly fellowship. Sometimes when I'm stressed and heavyhearted, I neglect those things when I need them the most.

Do you need some strength and encouragement today? Open your Bible, seek the Lord in prayer, and call a Christian friend.

For Further Thought

Why not memorize Psalm 28:7 and recite it whenever you start to feel weak?

> The LORD is my strength and my shield;
> my heart trusts in him, and I am helped.
> Therefore my heart celebrates,
> and I give thanks to him with my song.

Dwelling in the House of the Lord Forever

The Twenty-third Psalm poetically praises God as our loving Shepherd. I memorized it as a child, and whenever I recite it, I feel a childlike comfort.

But this psalm became my forever favorite the day I recited it at my mother's bedside. She was in the hospital in the final stages of cancer and on strong pain medication. I'd been praying for her and decided to quietly speak the words of Psalm 23 out loud in the King James Version, as I'd learned it.

> The LORD is my shepherd; I shall not want. He maketh me to lie down in green pastures: he leadeth me beside the still waters. He restoreth my soul.

It brought tears to my eyes when I heard my mother's voice joining in. Ever so softly she recited, "He leadeth me in the paths of righteousness for his name's sake." She wasn't awake, but the words of the psalm were hidden in her heart. Like me, she had memorized them as a child.

When she said, "Yea, though I walk through the valley of the shadow of death, I will fear no evil: for thou art with me; thy rod and thy staff they comfort me," she was walking through that valley. A few weeks later my mother met her Shepherd face-to-face. Surely goodness and mercy had followed her all the days of her life, and she is now dwelling in the house of the Lord forever.

If you've never memorized the Twenty-third Psalm, I encourage you to do so. The comfort it brings is indescribable.

For Further Thought

What practical things can we learn about our relationship with the Lord when we see Him as our Shepherd?

What Is Man?

Have you ever met a kind man married to an unkind woman or an honest woman married to a dishonest man? When we see unevenly matched relationships, we sometimes wonder what the godly person sees in their ungodly partner.

In Psalm 8:3–4, David asks God about a different type of relationship that is unevenly matched: "When I observe your heavens, the work of your fingers, the moon and the stars, which you set in place, what is a human being that you remember him, a son of man that you look after him?"

David was marveling at the glory of the heavens, and it made him wonder why such a magnificent Creator had placed such significance and privilege on sinful mankind. Hadn't God created a perfect world (Gen. 1)? Hadn't mankind messed it up (Gen. 3)? Hasn't God repeatedly forgiven men and nations for their ungrateful, arrogant unbelief? Hasn't He continued to offer us salvation? Yes, men and women have been mocking and rejecting God's love ever since the fall. Why does our gracious God continue to love us?

We should all be in awe that the Creator of the moon and stars would offer us His fatherly love. Sadly, modern man is

29

more likely to shake his fist at God and ask why He doesn't do more. But David's question should be our question too. And it should inspire us to praise our Lord every day for the favor He has shown mankind and for the love He has shown us personally.

For Further Thought

People who think they deserve God's love and salvation have not understood the gospel. In truth, Christ gives us what we don't deserve and can't earn. Titus 3:4–5 and Ephesians 2 offer additional insights.

Precious Predictions of Christ

I love how God whispered clues about Christ's coming throughout the entire Old Testament. These wonderful prophecies prove the supernatural and purposeful actions of God in human history. Psalm 22 is one example. It contains vivid descriptions of Christ's crucifixion: "I am poured out like water, and all my bones are disjointed; . . . my tongue sticks to the roof of my mouth. . . . They pierced my hands and my feet. . . . People look and stare at me" (vv. 14–17).

Look at these stunning comparisons below:

Psalm 22:1: "My God, my God, why have you abandoned me?"

Matthew 27:46: "About three in the afternoon Jesus cried out with a loud voice, *'Eli, Eli, lema sabachthani?'* that is, 'My God, my God, why have you abandoned me?'"

Psalm 22:7–8: "Everyone who sees me mocks me; they sneer and shake their heads: 'He relies on the LORD; let him save him; let the LORD rescue him, since he takes pleasure in him.'"

Matthew 27:39, 43: "Those who passed by were yelling insults at him, shaking their heads. . . . 'He trusts in God; let God rescue him now—if he takes pleasure in him!'"

Psalm 22:18: "They divided my garments among themselves, and they cast lots for my clothing.

Matthew 27:35: "After crucifying him, they divided his clothes by casting lots."

Beginning in Genesis 3:15, God planted "clues" about the coming of our Savior. He wants us to know that all along He had a plan to turn our darkness to light and our death to life. Thousands of years before Christ came to earth, Psalm 22 told us about His sacrificial death for our sins.

Isn't it wonderful to know that God's love for us is present in every detail of His revelation?

For Further Thought

Enjoy this prophecy of Christ's eternal sonship and priesthood: Psalm 2:7; Psalm 110; Acts 13:33; and Hebrews 5:1-10.

Unloading and Reloading

Sorrow, confusion, frustration, anger, fear, hopelessness—negative emotions can be our undoing if we don't handle them constructively. Psalms gives us some wonderful examples for dealing with discouragement biblically. It's what I call "unloading and reloading."

Repeatedly throughout the Psalms, the psalmists unload negative thoughts and feelings and reload, restore, refresh, and refocus their thoughts on God's love and faithfulness. For example, I can feel negative at times because God is so often misrepresented and maligned in our modern culture. Like Asaph in Psalm 74:10, I feel like asking, "God, how long will the enemy mock? Will the foe insult your name forever?"

But Asaph also shows me how to reload when he reminds himself that "God my King is from ancient times, performing saving acts on the earth" (v. 12). We may be tested by the negative pressures of culture, but our God is still in control. When Asaph says, "Rise up, God, champion your cause!" (v. 22), he knows our God is able to do that.

Another example is Psalm 86 where David unloads by admitting he feels "poor and needy" (v. 1). He's being attacked by arrogant people, and he has concerns about his own faithfulness. Have you ever felt that way? If so, you can reload as David did by saying, "You, Lord, are kind and ready to forgive, abounding in faithful love to all who call on you" (v. 5).

Many of the psalms follow this pattern of unloading negative emotions and reloading truths about God's character. It's a good practice for all of us.

For Further Thought

How does Romans 12:2 (AMP) confirm the truth of unloading and reloading? How does it offer a more permanent solution?

> And do not be conformed to this world [any longer with its superficial values and customs], but be transformed and progressively changed [as you mature spiritually] by the renewing of your mind [focusing on godly values and ethical attitudes], so that you may prove [for yourselves] what the will of God is, that which is good and acceptable and perfect [in His plan and purpose for you].

How Do You Feel about God's Word?

The psalmist who wrote Psalm 119 had a deep love and respect for God's Word. It's evident throughout this longest chapter in the Bible, and it should make us ask ourselves some relevant questions:

Psalm 119:24: "Your decrees are my delight and my counselors."

Do we delight in God's Word and seek its counsel?

Psalm 119:86: "All your commands are true; people persecute me with lies—help me!"

Do we trust God's Word even when it brings us mistreatment or persecution?

Psalm 119:89: "LORD, your word is forever; it is firmly fixed in heaven."

Do we understand how relevant, applicable, permanent, and unchanging it is?

Psalms 119:97: "How I love your instruction! It is my meditation all day long."

Do we love pondering it throughout our day?

Psalm 119:104: "I gain understanding from your precepts; therefore I hate every false way."

Do we consult it before making decisions?

Psalm 119:127: "I love your commands more than gold, even the purest gold."

Do we love it more than earthly treasures?

Psalm 119:136: "My eyes pour out streams of tears because people do not follow your instruction."

Do we hate seeing it mocked and denied?

Dear Lord, may we fully understand the power and beauty of Your Word.

For Further Thought

Psalm 119 is an acrostic poem, divided into twenty-two sections, each beginning with a letter in the Hebrew alphabet. I encourage you to read through this wonderful psalm, listing each attribute and each benefit of God's Word. Because most Bibles show these twenty-two sections, you can work though one section at a time.

Do We Become What We Think?

Repeat an error often enough, and it's eventually accepted as true. That's the case with teachings based on this single phrase in Proverbs 23:7: "As he thinketh in his heart, so is he" (KJV).

Self-esteem teachers use the phrase to claim we must think highly of ourselves because our view of ourselves determines the person we become. Others use this phrase to claim that our words superstitiously affect our health. Even some well-meaning Bible teachers misapply this phrase to reinforce the principle found in Philippians 4:8.

However, to come to any of these conclusions, you must quote a single phrase, not the whole verse, and you must quote it only in the King James Version.

Let's look at the full context: "Eat thou not the bread of him that hath an evil eye, neither desire thou his dainty meats: For as he thinketh in his heart, so is he: Eat and drink, saith he to thee; but his heart is not with thee. The morsel which thou hast eaten shalt thou vomit up, and lose thy sweet words" (Prov. 23:6–8 KJV).

This passage explains that a stingy person is always thinking about the cost of the food he serves others. It has nothing to do with the benefits of positive thoughts.

Our thoughts can affect our attitudes, but they don't change who we are. And they don't prevent or produce our healing. Both of those beliefs are superstitious, based on pulling a single phrase out of context.

For Further Thought

Please read Proverbs 23:6–8 in a number of different translations for further clarity. How do Proverbs 11:2 and Proverbs 15:33 refute the belief that we become better people if we speak highly of ourselves?

The Main Priority

David committed serious sins, and his words in Psalm 51 are an excellent example of sincere repentance. He understood that forgiveness was only possible through God's grace, love, and compassion: "Be gracious to me, God, according to your faithful love; according to your abundant compassion" (v. 1).

In verse 4, David made this statement: "Against you—you alone—I have sinned and done this evil in your sight." David wasn't denying he'd sinned against others. He was stating the "bottom-line" cause of his sin. When Nathan confronted David, he said David had "despised the LORD's command" and treated the Lord with "contempt" (2 Sam. 12:9, 14).

We know David sinned against Bathsheba, Uriah, and many others, but these sins were all symptoms of his sin against the Lord. Joseph also expressed this priority in Genesis 39:1-10. When Potiphar's wife tempted Joseph, he refused, explaining that Potiphar trusted him and saying, "How could I do this immense evil, and how could I sin against God?" (v. 9).

Every sin is a sin against God's character, His commands, and His love. David understood this truth, grieved that he had damaged his fellowship with the Lord, and fully repented to restore his most important relationship.

When you sin against others, do you realize you are sinning against God?

For Further Thought

God forgave David, but He also punished him for his sins. David responded without excuse, accepting both God's forgiveness and God's punishments (2 Sam. 12:1–23). He expressed his acceptance in Psalm 51:4: "You are right when you pass sentence; you are blameless when you judge." David's genuine repentance and his acceptance of God's just punishments set him apart. That is why God continued to compare other kings to David and why Scripture refers to David as "a man after God's heart" (see 1 Kings 11:4; 2 Kings 14:3; 15:3; Acts 13:22).

Standing Daily at God's Door

When I became a Christian in my early twenties, the Bible came alive for me. Even though I had two little ones in diapers and a soldier husband with a demanding schedule, I couldn't wait for my children's nap time so I could steal away and read God's Word.

Proverbs 8 personifies God's wisdom as a woman calling out to us: "People, I call out to you; . . . Anyone who listens to me is happy, watching at my doors every day, waiting by the posts of my doorway. For the one who finds me finds life and obtains favor from the LORD" (vv. 4, 34–35).

How well that expressed my feelings. I wanted to stand at the door of God's Word every day, seeking His counsel and advice. I'd had my fill of "philosophy and empty deceit based on human tradition" (Col. 2:8), and it was so refreshing to read God's words, knowing that none of them were "deceptive or perverse" (Prov. 8:8). I was beginning to apply biblical principles to my life and seeing the "knowledge and discretion" they brought (Prov. 8:12).

This delight in God's Word not only empowered my new relationship with the Lord, but it has sustained it throughout the years.

How happy is the one who does not walk in the advice of the wicked or stand in the pathway with sinners or sit in the company of mockers! Instead, his delight is in the LORD's instruction, and he meditates on it day and night. (Ps. 1:1–2)

For Further Thought

On a scale of one to ten, how would you describe your love for God's Word? If it's below ten, how might these Scriptures inspire a deeper appreciation: Psalm 19:7; Psalm 119:105, 130; Proverbs 30:5?

God's Unseen Footprints

I've moved more than twenty times since I've been married, and one thing I've learned is that moves rarely go as smoothly as planned. But one move was especially meaningful to us.

We felt sure God had called us to a new location to do ministry, so we set the date to vacate our rental house, packed up our belongings, and reserved a moving truck. But when we arrived to pick up the truck, it wasn't available, and there wasn't another truck available in the whole city that day. The situation seemed impossible.

In the Bible, the Israelites faced a much more serious "moving" problem. They were leaving captivity in Egypt, pursued by angry Egyptians. With the army at their back and the Red Sea in front, they had nowhere to go. Their situation seemed impossible.

God planned this "impossible" challenge to show them that nothing is impossible for Him. Psalm 77:19 explains God's plan: "Your way went through the sea and your path through the vast water, but your footprints were unseen." When everything seemed impossible, God parted the Red

Sea. His "footprints" beneath the sea weren't visible until the Israelites crossed through on dry ground.

Our moving problem was small in comparison but still important to us. As we were wondering what to do, a friend who lived hundreds of miles away unexpectedly pulled into our driveway. He just happened to be driving an empty truck headed close to our new destination. What a joy it was for us to see God's hidden "footprints."

For Further Thought

Suppose our friend had not shown up. How could Romans 8:28 (AMP) have given us comfort?

> And we know [with great confidence] that God [who is deeply concerned about us] causes all things to work together [as a plan] for good for those who love God, to those who are called according to His plan *and* purpose.

Are You Listening to the Sky?

It whispers snowflakes and hums soft winds. It shouts hailstorms and screams tornadoes. It proclaims sparkling sunshine and puffs white billowing clouds. It sings symphonies of darkness accented with moonbeams and twinkling stars. It murmurs, cries, and surprises us in bright blue, crimson red, and orange. It reminds us of man's sin and God's mercy with unexpected rainbows. It softly sprinkles refreshment to the dry soil, flashes warnings, and swirls soft melodies.

> The heavens declare the glory of God, and the expanse proclaims the work of his hands. Day after day they pour out speech; night after night they communicate knowledge. There is no speech; there are no words; their voice is not heard. Their message has gone out to the whole earth, and their words to the ends of the world. (Ps. 19:1-4)

God's creation testifies that we serve an omnipotent, omniscient, almighty God. The heavens were no cosmic accident; they were designed to tell us that our God exists and is filled with glory.

> For his invisible attributes, that is, his eternal power and divine nature, have been clearly seen since the creation of the world, being understood through what he has made. (Rom. 1:20)

The sky also gives us a "measure" of the greatness of our God's love: "For as high as the heavens are above the earth, so great is his faithful love toward those who fear him" (Ps. 103:11).

The skies speak of God's power, goodness, wisdom, love, and salvation. Are you listening?

For Further Thought

Notice how Psalms 8:1; 50:6; and 97:6 echo this truth.

Better than Any Sweepstakes

People enter sweepstakes all the time, hoping to win huge cash prizes even though their chances of winning are sometimes one in a billion. But one treasure is far better than any sweepstakes, and it's freely available to us. I'm talking about the treasure of God's Word.

In chapters 8 and 9, Proverbs personifies wisdom as a woman, but it's not referring to human wisdom. It's referring to God's wisdom found in His Word. Proverbs 3:14 and 8:10–11 explain that nothing equals the value of God's instructions, wisdom, and knowledge. They are more valuable than silver, gold, and jewels.

Persecuted Christians are willing to sacrifice life and livelihood to read their Bibles. They understand better than most of us the value of biblical wisdom and understanding (Prov. 16:16). Their sacrifices should be a reminder to us to daily open God's Word and rejoice in the fact that it is freely available. It's a treasure far beyond anything the world offers us, and we must not take it for granted.

We don't need to enter a sweepstakes or wait for someone to knock on our door with a million-dollar check. Instead, we can knock on God's door anytime day or night and receive His truths, which are beyond value (Prov. 8:34).

For Further Thought

Compare the treasures listed in Psalm 19:7–11 with the treasures mentioned in 1 John 2:15–17. Which of these lists best describes your values in life?

> The instruction of the LORD is perfect,
> renewing one's life;
> the testimony of the LORD is trustworthy,
> making the inexperienced wise.
>
> The precepts of the LORD are right,
> making the heart glad;
> the command of the LORD is radiant,
> making the eyes light up.
>
> The fear of the LORD is pure,
> enduring forever;
> the ordinances of the LORD are reliable
> and altogether righteous.
>
> They are more desirable than gold—
> than an abundance of pure gold;
> and sweeter than honey
> dripping from a honeycomb.
>
> In addition, your servant is warned by them,
> and in keeping them there is an abundant reward.
> (Ps. 19:7–11)

Plastic Faces, Pure Hearts

In the past few decades, plastic surgery has increased dramatically. People are resculpting their faces and other body parts in hopes of looking younger, prettier, or more handsome. Sadly, this trend represents the high value we place on outward appearance. If only we understood that inner beauty is more praiseworthy than external beauty.

Proverbs 31:30 has never been more relevant: "Charm is deceptive and beauty is fleeting, but a woman who fears the LORD will be praised." This is true for both men and women. The Amplified Bible adds some additional insights: "Charm *and* grace are deceptive, and [superficial] beauty is vain, But a woman who fears the LORD [reverently worshiping, obeying, serving, and trusting Him with awe-filled respect], she shall be praised."

We can look in a mirror and see the condition of our faces, but our heart is reflected in the mirror of God's Word (James 1:22–25). And our heart is where our beauty or ugliness shines forth: "As water reflects the face, so the heart reflects the person" (Prov. 27:19).

A heart filled with the joy of the Lord makes us more beautiful inside and out. As Proverbs 15:13 says, "A joyful heart makes a face cheerful."

Our ability to change our outward appearance is limited. We can't completely erase the signs of aging. But we can continually improve our inward beauty by seeking the Lord in every area of our lives. In fact, we can grow more beautiful as we age.

For Further Thought

How do these passages add to the truths in this devotion: Proverbs 11:22; 1 Samuel 16:7; and 1 Peter 3:3–4?

Taking Our Thoughts Captive

In Psalm 77, Asaph was so distressed he couldn't sleep. He'd been crying all night, feeling as if God had rejected him. But he was a man of faith, and he didn't allow himself to stay in this pit of despair. He began taking his thoughts captive by remembering God's character:

1. God is perfect in all His ways (v. 13).

   "God, your way is holy. What god is great like God?"

2. He can do anything (v. 14).

   "You are the God who works wonders; you revealed your strength among the peoples."

3. He redeems (v. 15).

   "With power you redeemed your people, the descendants of Jacob and Joseph."

4. He's the mighty ruler over all things (vv. 16–18).

"The water saw you, God. The water saw you; it trembled. Even the depths shook. The clouds poured down water. The storm clouds thundered; your arrows flashed back and forth. The sound of your thunder was in the whirlwind; lightning lit up the world. The earth shook and quaked."

5. He guides His people in unique ways (vv. 19–20).

"Your way went through the sea and your path through the vast water, but your footprints were unseen. You led your people like a flock by the hand of Moses and Aaron."

When we're distressed, we can follow the example of Asaph, taking our thoughts captive by pondering God's character and remembering His consistent faithfulness in our lives.

For Further Thought

We demolish arguments and every proud thing that is raised up against the knowledge of God, and we take every thought captive to obey Christ. (2 Cor. 10:5)

Glory to God, Not Man

Ever since the fall of man in Genesis 3, the world approaches life with upside-down priorities, esteeming man instead of God. Sadly, Psalm 139:14 is one of the passages sometimes misused for this purpose: "I will praise you because I have been remarkably and wondrously made. Your works are wondrous, and I know this very well."

Some popular teachers claim this verse encourages us to regularly tell ourselves and others how awesome we are. They claim we must highly esteem ourselves if we want to fulfill God's purposes. However, to get this meaning from Psalm 139:14, we must cut this verse in half, take it out of context, and ignore the main message of the psalm.

David isn't boasting about himself. He's boasting about our awesome Creator whose wisdom and love are beyond description. He ends the psalm with words that show humility, not pride: "Search me, God, and know my heart; test me and know my concerns. See if there is any offensive way in me; lead me in the everlasting way" (vv. 23–24). This is the attitude we need to fulfill God's purposes.

God loves us, but He didn't create us to worship ourselves. He created us to worship Him. If we look at God's design of the human body, mind, and soul and give ourselves credit, we've missed the point. Scripture teaches us to esteem God, not ourselves.

For Further Thought

Psalm 100:3 and Isaiah 64:8 complement the message of Psalm 139:14 and put man and God in proper perspective.

> Acknowledge that the LORD is God.
> He made us, and we are his—
> his people, the sheep of his pasture. (Ps. 100:3)

> Yet LORD, you are our Father;
> we are the clay, and you are our potter;
> we all are the work of your hands. (Isa. 64:8)

Standing Firm in Our Anti-Christian Culture

When our culture denies God's design and mocks His loving commands, we can identify with the question the psalmist asks in Psalm 11:3: "When the foundations are destroyed, what can the righteous do?" But Psalm 11 doesn't stop there. It goes on to give us inspiration and hope.

Verse 4 tells us that God is still on His throne. His truth will ultimately prevail. We can be sure that God sees all that is happening. He knows how evil mankind can be. He knows how strongly Christianity is ridiculed, mocked, and denied.

Verse 5 promises that God sees our righteous actions. He recognizes our faithfulness when we stand firm despite ridicule and mockery. He not only recognizes it; Matthew 5:10–11 tells us He rewards those who are mistreated for their faith.

The psalmist assures us that God passionately hates wickedness. He is perfectly patient and loving, but He is also perfectly just. Romans 1:18–32 describes this conflict between our holy God and ungodly mankind. It assures us that God's justice will eventually prevail (Ps. 11:6–7).

And the final words of Psalm 11 cannot help but give us courage: "For the LORD is righteous; he loves righteous deeds. The upright will see his face" (v. 7).

Things don't always make sense to us here on earth, but we have this wonderful promise: "Now we see only a reflection as in a mirror, but then face to face. Now I know in part, but then I will know fully, as I am fully known" (1 Cor. 13:12).

For Further Thought

How does 2 Corinthians 4 answer the question, "When the foundations are destroyed, what can the righteous do?"

The Sheer Delight of Psalm 1

Psalm 1 tells us the key to righteousness is a delight in God's Word.

> How happy is the one who does not walk in the advice of the wicked or stand in the pathway with sinners or sit in the company of mockers! Instead, his delight is in the LORD's instruction, and he meditates on it day and night. (Ps. 1:1-2)

Delight in God's Word always starts with a delight in God Himself—a deep desire to know Him with our whole being. As Paul describes in Philippians 3:7-14, it is "the surpassing value of knowing Christ Jesus my Lord" (v. 8). When we have that kind of delight in our Lord, we see Bible reading as an adventure, not a duty. Scripture verses come to our mind throughout the day to guide our thoughts and direct our choices. When we awaken in the night, we remember verses of Scripture as we drift back to sleep (Ps. 1:2).

Those who delight in God and His Word also delight in doing His will. There's nothing better than being "like a tree planted beside flowing streams that bears its fruit in its season" (Ps. 1:3)—nourished by living water, fulfilling God's purposes for our lives.

Delighting in God's Word gives us a deep assurance that God is guiding us and watching our steps (Ps. 1:6). The best part is this: if we don't have this delight in God's Word, all we have to do is ask. God is eager to give it (Matt. 7:7–11).

For Further Thought

I encourage you to go through Psalm 119, and each time you see the word "delight," note what delights the psalmist.

Why Would We Hide It?

Ionce taught a Bible study to a woman who was learning English as her second language.

I read Psalm 119:11 (NIV), "I have hidden your word in my heart that I might not sin against you," and before I could explain the meaning, she asked why we would want to hide God's Word. Great question.

Typically, we think of hiding as a way of concealing something from others, something we're ashamed of or some treasure we don't want to share. But Psalm 119:11 isn't talking about concealment. Quite the opposite. The Hebrew word for "hide" (*tsaphan*) is used in this verse to mean "treasure up." When we realize that God's Word is like pure gold for our souls, we cannot help but treasure it and want it stockpiled in our hearts (Ps. 119:127).

We want it to be more than an external influence. We want Scripture to become part of our being so it shines out of us in everything we do and everything we say. Then, as the psalmist explains, it will keep us from sinning against the Lord.

So, how do we hide Scripture in our hearts? We regularly read, study, memorize, and recite it. Then when we need direction, comfort, or encouragement, we can depend on all that we've "hidden" to fill our thoughts with biblical instruction, guidance, warning, and comfort.

Are you hiding God's Word in your heart or hiding it on an unused bookshelf?

For Further Thought

Years ago, I discovered that "hiding God's Word in my heart" could help me deal with my sins. I look for Scriptures dealing with a sin I'm struggling to overcome, write pertinent verses on three-by-five cards, and go over the verses several times a day, meditating on their wisdom. It sounds simplistic, but when we're sincere, it works. That's because the Bible is alive, accomplishing God's purposes, changing those who dwell on it (Heb. 4:12; Isa. 55:10–11; Col. 3:16).

Whose Heart Are You Going to Trust?

Trust your heart!" How often have you heard that phrase? Sadly, it's popularity is not based on wisdom. Many people who trust their hearts end up in destructive relationships, unethical business practices, and even in jail.

Proverbs 28:26 says, "He who trusts in his own heart is a fool, but whoever walks wisely will be delivered" (NKJV).

We find the reason for this warning in Jeremiah 17:9: "The heart is more deceitful than anything else, and incurable—who can understand it?" Jesus also warns us that "out of people's hearts, come evil thoughts, sexual immoralities, thefts, murders, adulteries, greed, evil actions, deceit, self-indulgence, envy, slander, pride, and foolishness. All these evil things come from within and defile a person" (Mark 7:21–23).

Our faith in Christ transforms our hearts and minds, but we're works in progress. Sometimes something "seems right," but it isn't (Prov. 14:12). That's why we must continually judge our desires and thoughts by comparing them to God's Word. Proverbs 3:5–6 is an important command:

"Trust in the LORD with all your heart, and do not rely on your own understanding; in all your ways know him, and he will make your paths straight."

Straight paths lead us to God's purposes (Eph. 2:10). So next time someone advises you to "trust your heart," let that be a cue to pick up your Bible and seek the Lord's "heart."

For Further Thought

Psalm 139:23–24 is a good prayer to pray before making decisions.

> Search me, God, and know my heart;
> test me and know my concerns.
> See if there is any offensive way in me;
> lead me in the everlasting way.

The Refreshment of Repentance

In Psalm 32, David explains the serious nature of unrepentant sin and the beauty of repentance.

When he refused to confess his sin, the stress of it affected his overall well-being: "When I kept silent, my bones became brittle from my groaning all day long. For day and night your hand was heavy on me; my strength was drained as in the summer's heat" (vv. 3–4).

The relief of confession was immediate: "Then I acknowledged my sin to you and did not conceal my iniquity. I said, 'I will confess my transgressions to the LORD,' and you forgave the guilt of my sin" (v. 5). What joy he experienced from the moment he sincerely repented of his sins: "How joyful is the one whose transgression is forgiven, whose sin is covered! How joyful is a person whom the LORD does not charge with iniquity and in whose spirit is no deceit!" (vv. 1–2).

A clean conscience keeps us in right relationship with the Lord, safe in His protection, "hidden" in His love, surrounded with joyful shouts: "You are my hiding place; you protect me from trouble. You surround me with joyful shouts of deliverance" (v. 7). This reference to joyful shouts reminds me of Luke 15:10 where Jesus talks about repentance that leads to salvation and the rejoicing there is in heaven over "one sinner who repents."

So let's not be stubborn (v. 9). Let's honestly confess our sins and enjoy the refreshment and joy it brings.

For Further Thought

Are there any sins you need to confess to the Lord?

If we say, "We have no sin," we are deceiving ourselves, and the truth is not in us. If we confess our sins, he is faithful and righteous to forgive us our sins and to cleanse us from all unrighteousness. If we say, "We have not sinned," we make him a liar, and his word is not in us. (1 John 1:8–10)

Don't Trivialize God's Name!

Have you ever heard someone call God "my biggest fan," "the man upstairs," or "my copilot"? We tend to give God names beneath Him.

The term *fan* is most often used for a sports or celebrity enthusiast or a person who greatly admires another. It's derived from the word *fanatic*, which means "extreme and often unreasonable zeal." God loves us deeply, but calling Him our fan puts Him in an inferior position.

The man upstairs . . . well, I don't think I need to explain why that name is unworthy of our almighty Creator God. And God is nobody's copilot. He flies the plane.

Why do we give God these trivial names? It's partly because we don't understand the majesty and wonder of our God. And a good way to improve our understanding of His character is to read the Psalms. For example, in the first two verses of Psalm 18, David calls God:

My Strength

My Rock

My Fortress

My Deliverer

My Shield

My Horn of Salvation

My Stronghold

These are wonderful names describing some of the many aspects of our glorious Lord. When we speak of God using names such as these, we bring Him glory, and we also remind ourselves of His awesome character. It's hard to remain fearful when we are praying to our Shield. It's hard to feel weak when we are praying to our Strength. It's hard to feel defeated when we are praying to our Deliverer.

For Further Thought

When you read through the Psalms, keep a list of names used for God. It's a wonderful way to ponder God's greatness and expand your prayer vocabulary.

Biblical "Rules of Speech"

Learning rules for grammar, punctuation, and sentence structure are important elements of our education. But even more important are the "rules of speech" found in Scripture, many of which are found in Proverbs.

For example, when someone says something rude, our natural tendency is to respond rudely. But Proverbs 15:1 offers this rule of speech: "A gentle answer turns away anger, but a harsh word stirs up wrath."

If we choose our words wisely, we'll find that people are more apt to listen to what we have to say, giving us better opportunities to share biblical truths. Proverbs 15:2 tells us that "the tongue of the wise makes knowledge attractive, but the mouth of fools blurts out foolishness." When a Christian humbly, carefully, and accurately shares God's truths, he or she "makes knowledge attractive."

An important contrast is noted in Proverbs 15:4: "The tongue that heals is a tree of life, but a devious tongue breaks the spirit." Christian speech should never be devious, exaggerated, or perverse. It shouldn't include mockery. Instead, our words should reflect the life-giving love and wisdom of our Lord. Even when God wants us to correct or rebuke someone, our words should flow from loving motives (Matt. 18:15; Gal. 6:1).

The New Testament reinforces these "rules of speech" in Ephesians 4 and 5, and the best summary is found in Ephesians 4:15, which tells us to "speak the truth in love" (NLT).

For Further Thought

Is there someone in your life who needs to hear God's truth spoken in love? Let these verses guide and encourage you: Psalm 141:5; Galatians 6:1; and 1 Thessalonians 5:14.

The Commands of a Loving Father

Psalm 119 is a song of love for God and His Word (v. 172). The psalmist beautifully describes the benefits and characteristics of Scripture, and he accurately sees God's commands as loving safeguards. We find this emphasis throughout the Psalms. And that's the emphasis Christians should have, especially in times when God's Word is distorted and denied.

When loving parents refuse to let their child run into traffic or eat candy all day, the child might think they are trying to spoil her fun. But we all know that children don't have as much knowledge and wisdom as their parents.

Similarly, God is our loving Father, and He's also our Creator who knows us better than we know ourselves. His commands are given for our protection, fulfillment, and well-being. Sadly, many in our world think they know more than God when it comes to things like sexual lifestyles, unborn life, honesty, integrity, wholesome entertainment, and so on. But their ignorance doesn't change the fact that

God's knowledge and wisdom are infinitely greater than human knowledge and wisdom.

Non-Christians often mock and deny God's Word (Rom. 1:16–32). And false teachers distort God's Word. But we fully trust God's commands because we know God's wise and loving character.

For Further Thought

Second Timothy 3:16–17 gives us a list of purposes of God's Word. Do you allow Scripture to do these things in your life?

> All Scripture is inspired by God and is profitable for teaching, for rebuking, for correcting, for training in righteousness, so that the man of God may be complete, equipped for every good work.

Weary from Grief

Each morning I woke up sad, and each night I went to bed sad. I couldn't conceal my grief. A major disappointment had knocked me down, and I was living in a pit of discouragement. I had let my sorrow overshadow my blessings.

I needed God desperately, but instead of spending more time in God's Word, I started spending less. And the less time I spent with God, the greater my sorrows, fears, and confusion became. I'm so glad that I finally came to my senses, realized my need, and began spending more time reading my Bible and praying.

I could have written Psalm 119:107: "I am severely afflicted; LORD, give me life according to your word." And God did just that. His Word began breathing life back into my emptiness and sorrow, and I was able to climb out of my pit of discouragement. Eventually, I could proclaim like the psalmist, "Trouble and distress have overtaken me, but your commands are my delight" (Ps. 119:143).

Since that time, when other difficulties knock me down, I've refused to slide back into a pit of despair and hopelessness. Whether I feel like it or not, I read Scripture and remind myself of God's character and purposes in my life. I have learned that when "I am weary from grief" God will strengthen me through His word (Ps. 119:28).

Have you learned this wonderful truth?

For Further Thought

How do Deuteronomy 8:3 and Matthew 4:4 highlight our need for daily time with God?

> He humbled you by letting you go hungry; then he gave you manna to eat, which you and your ancestors had not known, so that you might learn that man does not live on bread alone but on every word that comes from the mouth of the LORD. (Deut. 8:3)

> He answered, "It is written: Man must not live on bread alone but on every word that comes from the mouth of God." (Matt. 4:4)

Bruised Berries

About fifteen years ago, I bought strawberries at a fruit market in a foreign country. I looked for the stand with the most beautiful berries and asked for a kilo. When I got home, I discovered the berries were moldy and mashed, not the beautiful ones I'd seen on display. Some of the locals explained that I needed to beware of dishonest vendors who scoop from a barrel below the counter.

I'm sure this vendor thought his dishonesty was no big deal, but the Lord disagrees. Proverbs tells us that we are better off poor than dishonest: "Better a little with righteousness than great income with injustice" (Prov. 16:8).

Psalms echoes this truth: "The little that the righteous person has is better than the abundance of many wicked people" (Ps. 37:16).

A merchant may think it's insignificant to put a finger on the scales, but it's not insignificant to God: "Differing weights are detestable to the LORD, and dishonest scales are unfair" (Prov. 20:23).

It's obvious that mankind has always had a problem with cheating and defrauding. And God is concerned about honesty, whether it's a kilo of berries or a million-dollar purchase. Jesus made this point in Luke 16:10: "Whoever is faithful in very little is also faithful in much, and whoever is unrighteous in very little is also unrighteous in much."

Let's carefully examine our hearts and repent of anything dishonest, no matter how small.

For Further Thought

Proverbs 16:11 explains that we serve a God who is interested in all of the details: "Honest balances and scales are the LORD's; all the weights in the bag are his concern." What other passages in Scripture (besides those mentioned in this devotion) emphasize God's interest in little things?

A Foolish Contradiction?

Proverbs 26:4–5 is a "divine riddle": "Do not answer a fool according to his folly, or you yourself will be just like him. Answer a fool according to his folly, or he will be wise in his own eyes" (NIV).

At first glance, it sounds contradictory, but it's not. It's a unique way of presenting contrasting and complementary principles so we can carefully think them through. Some fools are filled with anger and mockery. They're not interested in truth. We can't shout into their self-deception without becoming angry and foolish ourselves. Other times, correcting foolishness is important, whether the fool listens or not. I've seen these two verses play out in these five ways in my life:

1. *Sometimes it's not our battle.* Scripture says we should be prepared to answer everyone (Col. 4:6). But it doesn't say we should answer everyone.
2. *Sometimes God tells us to respond with His truth.* Just as God told Ezekiel to speak His truth even if no one listens, there are times we must correct false teachings no matter the results (Ezek. 2:1–7).

3. *Sometimes enough is enough.* If I've repeatedly explained what Scripture teaches and the person repeatedly rejects it, it's probably time to step back and just pray for them (Titus 3:9–11).

4. *Sometimes the argument has no purpose.* It's what 2 Timothy 2:23–24 calls "foolish and ignorant disputes" that God's children should avoid.

5. *Timing matters.* People are more apt to listen when approached at the right time and the right place (Prov. 27:14).

So, when we encounter a foolish argument, let's choose which verse applies.

For Further Thought

Consider these instructions from 2 Timothy 2:23–25: "But reject foolish and ignorant disputes, because you know that they breed quarrels. The Lord's servant must not quarrel, but must be gentle to everyone, able to teach, and patient, instructing his opponents with gentleness."

Psalm 12 for Today

When God inspired David to write Psalm 12, I'm sure David didn't realize how relevant his words would be to people hundreds of years later, people like you and me. David describes some sad and trying times as people seek to be lord of their own lives. He feels like all is lost: "Help, LORD, for no faithful one remains; the loyal have disappeared from the human race" (v. 1).

When I look around at what's happening in our world, I sometimes feel the same. I can identify when David complains that the wicked "prowl all around" when worthless things are "exalted by the human race" (v. 8). This verse aptly describes our present culture. An increasing number of people are taking pride in soul-damaging behavior, celebrating things God forbids. Romans 1:32 puts it this way: "Although they know God's just sentence—that those who practice such things deserve to die—they not only do them, but even applaud others who practice them."

The world often discredits God's loving decrees, calling them outdated and even hateful. The opposite is true. When people experience the wisdom and protection of obeying

God, they cannot help but love and delight in all of God's commands (Ps. 119:40–47).

> The words of the LORD are pure words, like silver refined in an earthen furnace, purified seven times. (Ps. 12:6)

For Further Thought

The books of Psalms and Proverbs use the word *wicked* ten to twenty times more often than most other books in the Bible. The Hebrew word for *wicked* means "someone who is guilty of crime, sin, and/or hostility toward God." Romans 8:7 explains wickedness this way: "The mindset of the flesh is hostile to God because it does not submit to God's law. Indeed, it is unable to do so."

Man Says, "Show Me!"

Man says, "Show me and I'll trust you."
God says, "Trust me and I'll show you."

—Unknown

Trust is the firm belief in the reliability, truth, ability, or strength of someone or something. We're understandably cautious in trusting some people, especially those who are strangers or people who've proven untrustworthy in the past. They may need to show us they can be trusted. Unfortunately, we often bring this same skepticism to our faith in God. It's the basis of every crisis of faith. When we feel God has let us down, instead of trusting His wisdom and love, we start questioning His character with our human reasoning.

How foolish we are to think we can judge our infinite, omniscient God with our finite knowledge and wisdom. Relying on our own understanding is like leaning on a broken guardrail at the top of a cliff. If we trust ourselves, we can expect to fall headlong into a pit of confusion and unbelief. Instead, we must trust God and hold tightly to His promises even when we don't see the immediate results. That's what faith is all about (Heb. 11:1).

There have been times in my life when I've been genuinely confused about things God has allowed, but I've learned that He'll show me all that I need to know in His time and in His way.

> Trust in the LORD with all your heart, and do not rely on your own understanding. (Prov. 3:5)

For Further Thought

When we're confused about the things God allows in our lives, we can find comfort in the fact that "Our LORD is great, vast in power; his understanding is infinite" (Ps. 147:5).

Home Is Where the Heart Is

We've all heard the saying, "Home is where the heart is." It's been the theme of poetry, music, and movies.

Perhaps I understand the truth of the saying better than some. You see, I've made more than forty moves in my life, living all over the United States and in two European countries. And every house, apartment, flat, government quarters, trailer, and condo has become a home because I'm with my loved ones, those people I treasure most.

But more importantly, I'm at home with my Lord no matter where I'm located in this world. If the Lord is the treasure of our hearts, His plans for us will be our home. I love the way the psalmist expresses this truth: "Better a day in your courts than a thousand anywhere else. I would rather stand at the threshold of the house of my God than live in the tents of wicked people" (Ps. 84:10).

When we know the Lord, we recognize that He is our fortress, our refuge, our place of safety. He blesses our home when His principles and purposes are honored. Yes, home is definitely a matter of the heart, not a matter of location, and our heart is at home with whatever we value and cherish most: "For where your treasure is, there your heart will be also" (Luke 12:34).

For Further Thought

What are some practical ways you can make your home like the house described in Proverbs 24:3–4?

> A house is built by wisdom,
> and it is established by understanding;
> by knowledge the rooms are filled
> with every precious and beautiful treasure.

"Judge-Not" Confusion

Satan is always looking for ways to silence Christians, which is why he's likely the culprit behind modern-day "judge-not confusion." Many nonbelievers take Matthew 7:1 out of context to shame and silence Christians, and they've convinced many Christians that "it's not our place to judge."

But Scripture contains a different message. It tells us the wrong way to judge and the right way to judge, and it gives us biblical criteria for judging people, circumstances, and teachings. That's one of many benefits of the book of Proverbs. It's filled with practical advice for making biblical judgments.

For example, Proverbs 22:24–25 tells us to judge companions: "Don't make friends with an angry person, and don't be a companion of a hot-tempered one, or you will learn his ways and entangle yourself in a snare." Another example is Proverbs 20:19, which warns us to identify (judge) gossips and avoid them.

Judging biblically means we identify ungodly influences and we unashamedly share God's loving warnings against sin (Rom. 1:16).

Matthew 7:1–5, the misused "judge not" passage, doesn't warn against judging. It warns against hypocritical judgment, and we find that warning in Proverbs 26:24 as well.

No one is impartial. Judgment is a necessary part of life, whether we're deciding if a food is healthy or a relationship is healthy. Scripture doesn't command us not to judge; it commands us to do it biblically, wisely, humbly, graciously, and purposefully.

For Further Thought

James 2:1–4, 12–13 warns against the wrong type of judgment, and these passages describe situations where Christians are commanded to judge: Matthew 18:15; 1 Corinthians 15:33; Ephesians 5:5–11; James 5:19–20. Sometimes the words *condemn* and *judge* are used interchangeably, but most Christians understand condemnation as God's final judgment. That's why Christians can still be judged, corrected, and rebuked, but they are no longer under condemnation (Gal. 6:1; Rev. 3:19; Rom. 8:1).

Will You Conform?

When culture accepts moral values that oppose the Bible, Christians face increased pressure to conform. The pressure is especially strong when a close friend or family member chooses an ungodly path and claims that our love must include acceptance of their lifestyle. But love and approval are not synonymous.

We can't approve of lifestyles that God disapproves of because we know God's commands "are righteous and altogether trustworthy" (Ps. 119:138; see also vv. 86, 172). If we genuinely care about people, we will warn them of sins that damage their hearts and souls.

We should continue to show them love and try to keep the lines of communication open, praying that they will see the importance of living according to God's wise and loving commands. Perhaps they will come to realize, as we do, that "every word of God is pure; he is a shield to those who take refuge in him" (Prov. 30:5).

Whenever we face rejection from loved ones, we can go to our Friend who is closer than any human being, a Friend who is always there for us (Prov. 18:24). We know the Lord will guide and protect us.

The fear of mankind is a snare, but the one who trusts in the Lord is protected. (Prov. 29:25)

For Further Thought

What do Proverbs 2:7 and Psalm 84:11 tell us about the protection and blessing of obedience to God's commands?

> He stores up success for the upright;
> He is a shield for those who live with integrity.
> (Prov. 2:7)

> For the LORD God is a sun and shield.
> The LORD grants favor and honor;
> he does not withhold the good
> from those who live with integrity. (Ps. 84:11)

Twelve Reasons to Be Grateful

Gratitude is often in short supply even though it's important to every aspect of our lives. It keeps us from wallowing in self-pity, helps us see the good in a bad situation, and actually improves our physical, emotional, and spiritual health.

In Psalm 33, the psalmist offers twelve reasons God's people should be grateful:

1. God's Word is right (v. 4).
2. All He does is trustworthy (v. 4).
3. He loves righteousness and justice (v. 5).
4. His unfailing love fills the earth (v. 5).
5. He is our Creator, and all He needs to do is speak things into existence (vv. 6–9).
6. He is against evil plans of men and nations (v. 10).
7. His plans will prevail (v. 11).
8. God's people are blessed (v. 12).
9. Nothing escapes the Lord's notice (vv. 13–15).
10. The Lord watches over those who fear Him (v. 18).

11. He is our help and shield (v. 20).
12. Those who trust Him will experience His unfailing love (v. 21).

Most people base gratitude on circumstances, but Christians are different. Even when things are going badly, believers can be thankful for the twelve reasons above and hundreds more related to the goodness of our Lord.

May your faithful love rest on us, LORD, for we put our hope in you. (Ps. 33:22)

For Further Thought

There are endless reasons to be grateful to God. I encourage you to make your own list and add something to it every day. These New Testament passages also instruct us to be grateful: Philippians 4:6–7; Colossians 2:6–7; and 1 Thessalonians 5:16–18.

Finding Our "Happy Place"

The everyday stresses of life can weigh me down at times. That's when I want to steal away to a "happy place" to refresh and renew my mind and find some peace. Do you ever feel that way?

Guess what? We Christians can do that whenever we want. And we don't even need to change our location. In fact, when we feel overwhelmed, it's a sign that we've left our "happy place" and ventured into life carrying our own burdens instead of casting them on the Lord (Ps. 55:22).

> Taste and see that the LORD is good. How happy is the person who takes refuge in him! (Ps. 34:8)

> How happy is the one you choose and bring near to live in your courts! We will be satisfied with the goodness of your house, the holiness of your temple. (Ps. 65:4)

> How happy are those who reside in your house, who praise you continually. (Ps. 84:4)

The Lord is our "happy place," and we have an open invitation to come to Him: "Come to me, all of you who are weary and burdened, and I will give you rest" (Matt. 11:28).

For Further Thought

Why not memorize one of the verses in this devotion so you can recite it when you are feeling overwhelmed and need to remember your "happy place."

The Desires of God's Heart

I saw this on the license plate of an expensive sports car: "Ps.37:4." Psalm 37:4 is a well-known verse, one that is often misunderstood and misused: "Take delight in the LORD, and he will give you your heart's desires." It's nice that this sports car owner acknowledged all things in life are blessings from God, but owning a sports car isn't the point of this verse.

Let me share how God made this verse real in my life and helped me understand the meaning. It happened when my husband was in the army, and we received orders for an undesirable assignment in an undesirable location. We were disappointed. But as we talked and prayed about it, we began to see God's hand in it. And we actually got excited. God had replaced *our* desires with *His* desires.

And that's the promise in this verse—first we delight ourselves in the Lord, in His plans, His thoughts, and His purposes. Soon we find that we have traded our selfish desires for His perfect desires. His heart's desire becomes our own.

There's nothing wrong with owning a sports car, but Psalm 37:4 is not about acquiring wealth or pleasure

(1 John 2:15–17). It's not about changed circumstances; it's about changed desires.

For Further Thought

How does the context of Psalm 37:4 help us better understand it?

> Trust in the LORD and do what is good;
> dwell in the land and live securely.
> Take delight in the LORD,
> and he will give you your heart's desires.
>
> Commit your way to the LORD;
> trust in him, and he will act,
> making your righteousness shine like the dawn,
> your justice like the noonday. (Ps. 37:3–6)

Self-Esteem or Self-Control?

The young girl was telling her father what an awesome soccer player she was going to be.

"You'll need to practice," her father said. "You've never played soccer before."

"I don't need to practice," she said confidently. "I'll be awesome just the way I am."

This is one of the many negative results of overpraising our children. This little girl's self-esteem had replaced her common sense. If she continues to think so highly of herself, she will never develop self-control or competency in a new skill like soccer.

This problem is not limited to children. It crosses cultural and generational boundaries. And it's a direct contradiction to God's Word:

> Proverbs 11:2: "When arrogance comes, disgrace follows, but with humility comes wisdom."

> Proverbs 27:2: "Let another praise you, and not your own mouth—a stranger, and not your own lips."

Proverbs 29:23: "A person's pride will humble him,
but a humble spirit will gain honor."

We find a similar warning in Luke 14:11: "For everyone who exalts himself will be humbled, and the one who humbles himself will be exalted."

Self-esteem teachings owe their popularity to our fallen human nature. We'd much rather build our self-esteem than our self-control even though self-control is preferable. When Galatians 5:22–23 lists the fruit of the Spirit, it includes self-control and does not include self-esteem. In fact, two verses after these qualities of Christian maturity are listed, we find this warning: "We must not become conceited" (v. 26 HCSB).

For Further Thought

Are there areas where you've accepted self-esteem teaching? Notice how Romans 12:3 confirms the words of Proverb 27:2.

What Are You Relying On?

In Numbers 13, God told Moses to have some men explore the land of Canaan, which He was giving them. This was a fact-finding mission because God had already promised to give them the land. Sadly, ten of the twelve leaders "relied on their own understanding." They treated their fact-finding mission as a fear-finding mission.

Were they exaggerating when they said that the people of Canaan were too strong for them? Probably not. But God wasn't asking them if they had the human strength and human wisdom to take the land. He'd already told them He'd give them the land. They needed to trust His strength and wisdom, not their own.

Their refusal to depend on the Lord cost that generation the promised land and resulted in a life of wilderness wandering. What an important warning for us.

There are times when the facts seem stacked against doing something we know the Lord wants us to do. When that happens, we can "lean on" our own understanding like the ten spies. Or we can obey Proverbs 3:5–6 as Caleb and Joshua did: "Trust in the LORD with all your heart, and do not rely on your own understanding; in all your ways know him, and he will make your paths straight."

Is there an area of your life where you've let your limited human understanding or your fear get in the way of God's promises?

For Further Thought

For a look at God's incredible patience with His people, read Psalm 106.

Listening When We Pray

Have you ever had someone ask you to counsel them in a particular area, but after several conversations you realized they weren't going to listen to your advice (Prov. 18:2)?

I've had this happen, and it reminds me how easy it is for any of us to resist godly counsel if we're not careful.

Psalm 50:16–21 addresses this problem, describing people who recite God's statutes but hate His instruction. It explains that they think God is like them because they've created a god who approves of everything they do.

When we go to the Lord in prayer, we need to understand who He is and who we are. "The LORD values those who fear him, those who put their hope in his faithful love" (Ps. 147:11). If we fear the Lord, we realize that His faithful love includes rebuke as well as comfort, correction as well as affirmation. The psalmists understood this. They understood the necessity of repenting of their sins:

> "If I had cherished sin in my heart, the Lord would not have listened." (Ps. 66:18 NIV)

They understood that only God could help them see their sins clearly:

> "Who perceives his unintentional sins? Cleanse me from my hidden faults." (Ps. 19:12)

They understood the beauty of being broken and humble before the Lord:

> "The sacrifice pleasing to God is a broken spirit. You will not despise a broken and humbled heart, God." (Ps. 51:17)

God is always available to listen to us, but we must be willing to listen to Him.

For Further Thought

Sometimes we pretend to listen, but we hear what we want to hear, not what we need to hear. This is similar to the problem explained in James 1:22–25. Are you resisting God's correction in any area of your life?

Pure in Our Own Eyes

Instead of honoring parents, our modern culture encourages us to judge them, deciding if they are "worthy" of our respect. This attitude isn't new. It's succinctly described in Proverbs 30:11-13:

> There is a generation that curses its father and does not bless its mother. There is a generation that is pure in its own eyes, yet is not washed from its filth. There is a generation—how haughty its eyes and pretentious its looks.

This is how God views those who speak harshly about their parents. If adult children cannot offer their parents grace, forgiveness, and consideration, this passage describes them as arrogant and cruel. We shouldn't be surprised because people who show contempt for their earthly parents also show contempt for God's commands.

God knows that all parents are imperfect human beings, and He knows that some are difficult and annoying. Yet He stresses honoring them throughout Scripture. Even if a parent is unworthy, we honor them out of respect for God's commands. Perhaps one reason God attached a promise to

this command is that He realizes it's not always easy to obey
(Eph. 6:2–3).

So let's ask God if He is pleased with the way we have
handled our relationship with our parents. Even if it is a good
relationship, let's consider ways we can improve it.

For Further Thought

Both Old and New Testaments emphasize our relationship with our parents. There are some strong warnings
in some of these passages: Exodus 20:12; Leviticus 20:9;
Deuteronomy 5:16; Proverbs 20:20; 30:17; Matthew 15:1–9;
Romans 1:28–32; 1 Timothy 5:4; and 2 Timothy 3:1–5.

*Note: This devotion is not addressing situations where a child
has been physically or sexually abused by a parent. Those
instances require special care.*

Exaggeration or Aggressive Pursuit?

It's become increasingly popular to exaggerate relationship problems, calling annoying people "toxic" and negative people "verbally abusive." Words that were previously used for serious mental and emotional problems are now used for normal relationship difficulties.

These hopeless descriptions may help us avoid the hard work of problem-solving and reconciliation, but they cause us to lose opportunities to develop healthy people skills. Misunderstandings and disagreements are part of life. If we refuse to deal with them, we never learn how to handle them biblically and constructively.

Instead of understanding the beauty of forgiveness, we'll keep bitter lists of past offenses to pull out whenever a problem arises, rejecting the wisdom in Proverbs 19:11: "A person's insight gives him patience, and his virtue is to overlook an offense."

Instead of learning self-control, we'll be easily angered, creating even more conflict in our relationships: "A hot-tempered person stirs up conflict, but one slow to anger calms strife" (Prov. 15:18).

Eventually we'll develop a "spiritual stinginess," a weakening of our souls, a loss of spiritual strength and wisdom, described in Proverbs 24:10: "If you falter in a time of trouble, how small is your strength!" (NIV).

That's why Scripture commands us to "seek peace and pursue it" (Ps. 34:14). The Hebrew word for "pursue" in this verse expresses an aggressive, ardent pursuit. So let's aggressively and ardently pursue peace in our relationships so we can grow up in our faith.

For Further Thought

Romans 12:9–21 is a good New Testament passage to apply to our relationships. Romans 12:18 echoes the truth in Psalm 34:14.

If You Have Breath

In the six short verses of Psalm 150, we find more than ten commands to praise God for "his powerful acts" and "his abundant greatness." The psalm commands vibrant, joyful praise using rams' horns, harps, lyres, tambourines, stringed instruments, flutes, and resounding cymbals. It suggests we praise the Lord with our voices and with dancing and singing. It's not mentioned in this psalm, but we can even praise God in our thoughts without speaking a word.

> Let everything that breathes praise the LORD. (Ps. 150:6)

Giving thanks is extremely important, but praise takes it up a notch. It's not simply thanking God for something He's done. It's thanking God for who He is. Psalm 100:4 says praise draws us right into the inner courts of God's presence: "Enter his gates with thanksgiving and his courts with praise. Give thanks to him and bless his name."

Old Testament saints could enter the courts of God's temple, but only the priests could go into the holy of holies and speak directly to the Lord. That's no longer true. Jesus brought us closer to God and gave us even more reasons to praise Him. He made us a chosen people, a royal priesthood (1 Pet. 2:9), and "we have boldness to enter the sanctuary through the blood of Jesus" (Heb. 10:19).

If you've got breath in your lungs, praise God daily for that privilege.

For Further Thought

Read through Psalm 100 and note the ways it highlights various aspects of our relationship with God: service, singing, thanksgiving, and praise. Does your spiritual life include these things?

He Collects Our Tears

In some ancient cultures people mourned the death of a loved one by collecting their tears in a bottle. It was a visible way to show their devotion and sorrow.

This custom is reflected in the figurative language of Psalm 56:8 (NLT):

> You keep track of all my sorrows. You have collected all my tears in your bottle. You have recorded each one in your book.

We shouldn't assume that God actually records each tear and puts it in a bottle, but it's a beautiful metaphor, a comforting word picture. It shows us the depth of God's concern because it doesn't depict us as collecting our own tears. It depicts God carefully collecting and recording them for us.

God is always present in our lives and fully aware of every detail, every tear, every sorrow, every fear, every emotion good or bad, past and present. In fact, He even knows what we'll face in the future.

He's not a busy, distant, impersonal God. He is ever present and fully aware of everything going on in our lives. So next time you are hurting, remember that the Lord is interested, understanding, and available.

No matter what is troubling us, we should "seek the LORD and his strength; seek his face always" (Ps. 105:4).

For Further Thought

Often our tears are a result of hardships that refine our faith, and we can be assured that "those who sow in tears will reap with shouts of joy" (Ps. 126:5). What does Revelation 21:3–4 tell us about sorrows that seem to have no resolution here on earth?

> Then I heard a loud voice from the throne: Look, God's dwelling is with humanity, and he will live with them. They will be his peoples, and God himself will be with them and will be their God. He will wipe away every tear from their eyes. Death will be no more; grief, crying, and pain will be no more, because the previous things have passed away.

Wisdom, Joy, and Radiance in Psalm 19

Until we make God's Word an integral part of our lives, we tend to underestimate its value. However, when we start reading and studying it regularly, we can agree with the psalmist in Psalm 19:7–10:

> "The instruction of the LORD is perfect, renewing one's life; the testimony of the LORD is trustworthy, making the inexperienced wise." (v. 7)
>
> *God's Word renews and refreshes our souls with perfect wisdom.*

> "The precepts of the LORD are right, making the heart glad." (v. 8)
>
> *Understanding the principles and purposes of our lives brings joy to our hearts.*

> "The command of the LORD is radiant, making the eyes light up." (v. 8)

Our spiritual vision improves as truth and error come to light.

"The ordinances of the LORD are reliable and altogether righteous." (v. 9)

We learn that God's Word is not like human words. It's completely trustworthy.

"[The ordinances] are more desirable than gold—than an abundance of pure gold." (v. 10)

The growth we experience from reading God's Word is beyond value.

"[They are] sweeter than honey dripping from a honeycomb." (v. 10)

God's Word becomes sweet and enjoyable to our souls, and we crave it.

When we read and study God's Word, we begin to experience it's powerful, purposeful, productive work in our lives.

Do you feel that you're giving God's Word the priority it deserves in your life?

For Further Thought

I encourage you to read Psalm 19 and notice the way David begins with the "wordless" wisdom of God in creation, moves to the specific benefits and descriptions of God's written Word, and ends with the appropriate response to God's Word.

What about Promises for Health and Protection?

Notice the promises in these two psalms:

Psalm 103:3: "He forgives all your iniquity; he heals all your diseases."

Psalm 121:7 (NIV): "The LORD will keep you from all harm—he will watch over your life."

Can Christians be assured we'll never be sick or harmed? What about the missionaries and other God-honoring people throughout history who suffered illness or mistreatment? What about Timothy who suffered from "frequent illnesses" (1 Tim. 5:23)? What about Paul who suffered great harm (2 Cor. 11:16–33)?

How do we handle passages like the two psalms above?

First, we need to understand that God made and fulfilled many earthly promises to the nation of Israel based on their obedience to His commands (e.g., Exod. 15:26). Many of these were not permanent but specific to that time and place in history. The psalms were written during this period.

Second, on the cross Christ completely conquered death, sickness, and Satan, but these things continue to bother us in our earthly lives (Isa. 53:5; John 16:33; 2 Cor. 5:1–10; Col. 2:13–15; Heb. 2:5–9).

Third, our finite minds can't fully grasp the ways of our infinite God. Healing and protection involve some mystery (Deut. 29:29). This may cause some to reject Him, but those of us who trust His character can wait for the answers (1 Cor. 13:12). Until then, we can rest in His faithful love (Ps. 36:7).

For Further Thought

Even though we don't experience the fullness of Christ's victory here on earth (Heb. 2:5–9), we are assured that our eternity with our Lord will be perfect, pain-free, and filled with peace. I encourage you to ponder that truth whenever you face difficulties.

My Secret Room

Mark is an engineer, and when he realized there was dead space beneath the stairs in his house, he decided to create a secret room for his children. They access it by climbing through a kitchen cabinet, and it's big enough for their dad to join them. How fun is that? It's meant to be a place to play, but it would also be a safe place to hide from an intruder.

I've always wanted a secret room, something accessed through a bookcase or hidden door. I'm not sure why I find this so appealing. Perhaps it's because I sometimes want to hide from all the worldly pressures.

Recently when I was struggling with some heavy problems, my friend Linda wrote to tell me that while she was praying for me, God brought Psalm 32:7 to her mind: "You are my hiding place; you protect me from trouble. You surround me with joyful shouts of deliverance."

There's something special about a friend who writes with a Scripture attached, and God used Linda that day to remind me of such an important truth: when life hurts, when we feel broken and bruised, we have a safe place to go, a place where we can lay down our sad thoughts and rest in the love of our Lord and Protector.

I am so glad that my Father thought to include a "secret room" in His love for me, a place of retreat and protection.

For Further Thought

How great is your goodness, which you have stored up for those who fear you. In the presence of everyone you have acted for those who take refuge in you. You hide them in the protection of your presence; you conceal them in a shelter from human schemes, from quarrelsome tongues. (Ps. 31:19–20)

Women Home Builders

Proverbs 14:1 uses a fitting metaphor for a woman's role in her family: "Every wise woman builds her house, but a foolish one tears it down with her own hands."

This reminds me of the saying, "If momma ain't happy, ain't nobody happy." It's a humorous statement, but it's similar to the message of Proverbs 21:19: "Better to live in a wilderness than with a nagging and hot-tempered wife." This truth is also found in Proverbs 21:9 and 25:24.

When God designed roles in the family, He gave the husband the role of leadership (Eph. 5:22–33), and He gave the wife the role of influence (1 Pet. 3:1–6). The husband has a powerful impact on his family, but the wife's influence is every bit as important.

Unbelieving husbands may be won over without a word by the way their wives live. It's not a promise, but a woman's gentle, submissive, inner beauty is a strong influence. She can set the tone in her marriage and in her home for good or bad, building it up or tearing it down.

When shaped by her faith in Christ, a wife's attitudes, actions, words, decisions, and priorities can soften the effects of a stressed husband, sick child, or unexpected crisis.

She can't right all the wrongs in a family. That's not her job. But she can create an atmosphere that is godly, warm, and loving.

For Further Thought

Whether you are a wife, a husband, a child at home, or a single adult, I encourage you to consider ways you might improve the atmosphere in your home. "Unless the LORD builds a house, its builders labor over it in vain" (Ps. 127:1).

Fake News and Faulty Sources

We definitely live in the "information age" with millions of facts at our fingertips. But we could just as accurately call it the "misinformation age" because we also have millions of lies at our fingertips. If you haven't heard a false rumor about politics, celebrities, climate, or health issues in the last week, you've probably been in a coma. Sometimes even respectable news agencies get taken in and have to post retractions.

The availability of online resources makes it easier for Christians to study God's Word. But it also makes it easier for Christians to find false teachings and slanderous articles about well-known Christian teachers, authors, and speakers. I love the way the book of Proverbs addresses this problem:

> The inexperienced one believes anything, but the sensible one watches his steps. (Prov. 14:15)

This is a good reminder to stop, pray, and check our facts before passing along the latest Bible teaching, latest conspiracy theory, latest political plot, or latest critique of a well-known leader. In addition, we should seek information from sources that are careful and gracious. God wants His people to be warned about false teachers, but we shouldn't trust sources that use sarcasm or mockery. If we pass along fake news or slander, we are just as guilty as those who started the rumors (Prov. 17:4).

So let's be prudent, dear Christian. Let's check our facts and use reliable sources.

For Further Thought

I will destroy anyone who secretly slanders his neighbor; I cannot tolerate anyone with haughty eyes or an arrogant heart. (Ps. 101:5)

They Think God Is Just Like Them

The idols of the nations are of silver and gold, made by human hands. . . . Those who make them are just like them, as are all who trust in them.

(Ps. 135:15, 18)

People who worship idols are "just like" their false gods—powerless, without wisdom, without truth.

This applies to mind-crafted idols as well. Whenever people rebel against the true and living God, they create and worship fake, useless gods. Paul talks of people in the early church preaching "another Jesus," and that still happens today when people deconstruct biblical truths and reconstruct a faith that fits their lifestyle and their human understanding (2 Cor. 11:3–4).

The Jesus they sculpt with their finite minds has little resemblance to the Jesus of Scripture. He's very accommodating. He approves popular sins, worldly values, and situational ethics. He never punishes anyone because he lets each person decide what is right and wrong. But this false Jesus is just like his creators. He is limited by their human wisdom, knowledge, and values.

Psalm 50:16–17, 21 records God's response to people who customize God in this way: "What right do you have to recite my statutes and to take my covenant on your lips? You hate instruction and fling my words behind you. . . . You thought I was just like you."

False versions of Jesus appeal to mankind's fallen human nature. They're easier to understand and manipulate than the real Jesus, but they cannot save anyone from sin.

For Further Thought

> I fear that, as the serpent deceived Eve by his cunning, your minds may be seduced from a sincere and pure devotion to Christ. For if a person comes and preaches another Jesus, whom we did not preach, or you receive a different spirit, which you had not received, or a different gospel, which you had not accepted, you put up with it splendidly! (2 Cor. 11:3–4)

In what ways do you see this passage playing out in our culture right now?

You Probably Don't Remember Me

I'd been in his seminary class with two hundred other students, so when I saw the professor several years later, I said, "You probably don't remember me, but I'm a former student."

That situation came to mind when I was reading Psalm 139. It tells us that even though we are one in more than seven billion world inhabitants, God knows our every move, our every thought, our every fear, our every joy (vv. 1–6).

> "LORD, you have searched me and known me. You know when I sit down and when I stand up; you understand my thoughts from far away. You observe my travels and my rest; you are aware of all my ways. Before a word is on my tongue, you know all about it, LORD. You have encircled me; you have placed your hand on me. This wondrous knowledge is beyond me. It is lofty; I am unable to reach it."

Verses 7–12 are similar to Romans 8:38–39, assuring us that nothing can separate us from God's presence.

Verses 13–16 praise God as our Creator, confirming the sanctity of unborn human life, telling us that God knits us together in our mother's womb and keeps His eye on us before we ever see the light of day. We are His creation. He has known us from the moment we were conceived. He knows every detail of our childhood and every fear of our adult years. He loves us, and He's always with us.

When we ponder these wonderful truths, we can easily repeat the praises of David in verse 6: "This wondrous knowledge is beyond me."

For Further Thought

What situations in your life help you understand God's constant presence?

> Where can I go to escape your Spirit? Where can I flee from your presence? If I go up to heaven, you are there; if I make my bed in Sheol, you are there. If I fly on the wings of the dawn and settle down on the western horizon, even there your hand will lead me; your right hand will hold on to me. If I say, 'Surely the darkness will hide me, and the light around me will be night'—even the darkness is not dark to you. The night shines like the day; darkness and light are alike to you. (Ps. 139:7–12)

Warnings against Sexual Sins

Large portions of Proverbs 5–7 are devoted to warnings against sexual sins.

> Can a man embrace fire and his clothes not be burned? Can a man walk on burning coals without scorching his feet? . . . The one who commits adultery lacks sense; whoever does so destroys himself. (Prov. 6:27–28, 32)

God created intimacy for a married man and woman, and He made it completely satisfying, healthy, and enriching: "Let your fountain be blessed, and take pleasure in the wife of your youth. A loving deer, a graceful doe—let her breasts always satisfy you; be lost in her love forever" (Prov. 5:18–19).

To deny God's design for sexual intimacy is to doubt His wisdom as our Creator. He alone knows what is healthy and good for our bodies and souls, and we ignore His warnings at great expense.

Sexual sins tend to take over a person's life, doing increasing damage. And approval of sexual sins can damage entire cultures and nations as well. We've seen this happening around the globe. Things that once shocked us have become commonplace. Things once hidden by a few are now celebrated by many.

Proverbs 14:12 is a fitting warning: "There is a way that seems right to a person, but its end is the way to death." How many men and women have destroyed families, careers, reputations, and ministries by getting involved in a sexual relationship that "seemed right" at the time?

May Christians lead the way in obeying and explaining God's loving commands.

For Further Thought

If you have violated God's commands, repent, seek His forgiveness, and find a mature Christian to hold you accountable. If you were involved in sexual immorality in the past, make sure you have genuinely repented and asked the Lord's forgiveness (1 John 1:8–10).

Unanswered Prayer

Have you ever prayed for something that seemed to be in accordance with God's will, but it didn't happen? We sometimes call this "unanswered prayer," but there's actually no such thing. That's just a term we use when God says "no" or "wait."

Over time, we often realize why God chose not to answer a specific request. I've known people who prayed that God would give them a particular spouse, and when it didn't happen, they felt God had let them down. Then, years later when they met and married their soulmate, they thanked God for that "unanswered" prayer.

But we don't always have that advantage. Sometimes we genuinely don't understand why our prayer wasn't part of God's will. That's when we remind ourselves that God is omniscient: "The eyes of the LORD are everywhere" (Prov. 15:3).

Our view is limited. As 1 Corinthians 13:12 says, "Now we see only a reflection as in a mirror, but then [when we meet Christ in heaven] face to face. Now I know in part, but then I will know fully, as I am fully known."

This side of heaven, we may not fully understand our "unanswered" prayers. Some of the things that seem so right to our human minds may have terrible consequences (Prov. 14:12; 16:25). That's why Proverbs 3:5 warns us not to trust ourselves but to put our wholehearted trust in the Lord who is all-knowing, all-wise, and perfectly loving.

For Further Thought

"Many are the plans in a person's heart, but it is the LORD's purpose that prevails" (Prov. 19:21 NIV). Have you seen the wisdom and purpose of an unanswered prayer in your life? How can 1 Corinthians 13:12 offer comfort when we don't understand why our prayers are not answered?

What Chains?

No nation, institution, or person can abandon God's laws without abandoning true freedom. We see this repeatedly played out in human history.

"Workers of the world unite; you have nothing to lose but your chains!" was the Marxist motto that promised a brave new world. Marxists promised they would bring equality and improved living standards to all people. In truth, they simply removed one set of chains and shackled the people with another set, and half of Europe suffered under dictatorial, God-hating Communist oppression for the next forty years.

Psalm 2:1–3 addresses this oft-repeated scenario:

> Why do the nations rage and the peoples plot in vain? The kings of the earth take their stand, and the rulers conspire together against the LORD and his Anointed One: "Let's tear off their chains and throw their ropes off of us."

Ever since the fall of man, there has been a struggle between God's truth and man-made philosophies and religions. We see this in human history, and we also see it in individual lives. Each of us must decide if we will choose human views of God and man or biblical views. We may think we'll find freedom in sidestepping the one true God, but that will only keep us in chains.

Why? Because Jesus is the only one who can set us free and "if the Son sets you free, you really will be free" (John 8:36).

For Further Thought

In Acts 4 Peter and John were taken into custody by the Jewish leaders for preaching and performing miracles in Christ's name. After they were released they joined the rest of believers in a prayer than included Psalm 2:1–2. I encourage you to read Acts 4 for a fuller understanding of this Psalm. In addition, you will find that Peter and John quoted another Psalm when being questioned by the Sanhedrin.

Three Powerful Truths in the Shortest Psalm

Psalm 117 is the shortest chapter in the Bible, just two verses, approximately twenty words. But the message is power packed.

> Praise the LORD, all nations! Glorify him, all peoples! For his faithful love to us is great; the LORD's faithfulness endures forever. Hallelujah!

There are three powerful truths in this short psalm:

1. *God deserves praise from all nations and all people.* In our fallen world, God doesn't get the adoration He deserves, but one day Christians "from every tribe and language and people and nation" will eternally sing about His glory (Rev. 5:9).

Have you taken time today to praise Him?

2. *God's love toward us exceeds all expectations.* Nothing compares to the love of the Lord: "For as high as the heavens are above the earth, so great is his faithful love toward those who fear him" (Ps. 103:11).

Have you ever pondered the fact that God's love for you is beyond measure?

3. *God's faithfulness "endures forever"—it's eternal.* God's faithfulness is like His love—beyond description: "For the LORD is good, and his faithful love endures forever; his faithfulness, through all generations" (Ps. 100:5).

Why not take some time today to remember examples of God's faithfulness in your life?

From beginning to end, Psalm 117 proclaims God's greatness, and it inspires us to do the same. It may be the shortest chapter in the Bible, but it proves the old adage that good things can come in small packages.

For Further Thought

Have you ever thought of writing a twenty-five-word psalm of praise to the Lord? Why not give it a try?

What's in a Name?

What does it mean to trust in a name?

When David said, "Some trust in chariots and some in horses, but we trust in the name of the LORD our God" (Ps. 20:7 NIV), he was talking about trusting God's power, purposes, and promises.

When he approached the giant Goliath, both the Israelites and Philistines thought he was trusting in his own name, but David set them straight:

> You come against me with a sword, spear, and javelin, but I come against you in the name of the LORD of Armies, the God of the ranks of Israel. (1 Sam. 17:45)

David's strength and slingshot skills could never have defeated Goliath unless they were part of the power, purposes, and promises of God.

There are times in our lives when we face Goliaths, and the circumstances seem stacked against us. However, if we are following God's lead and moving forward in His name, nothing will stop us except our own doubts.

Those who know your name trust in you because you have not abandoned those who seek you, LORD. (Ps. 9:10)

And how do we "know" God's name? By spending time in His Word and in prayer and fellowship, growing in our faith. Then we will reach the point where we can say, "In him our hearts rejoice, for we trust in his holy name" (Ps. 33:21 NIV).

For Further Thought

When God guides you to do something that seems beyond your strength or ability, open your Bible and read Psalm 28:7: "The LORD is my strength and my shield; my heart trusts in him, and I am helped. Therefore my heart celebrates, and I give thanks to him with my song." It's a good verse to memorize.

Feeling Forgotten

I went through an especially dark time in my life when I felt God had forgotten me. I could identify with the emotions David expressed in Psalm 13:1–2: "How long, Lord? Will you forget me forever? How long will you hide your face from me? How long will I store up anxious concerns within me, agony in my mind every day? How long will my enemy dominate me?"

I was definitely storing up my anxious concerns during the day and even waking in the middle of the night feeling troubled, forgotten, wondering why God wasn't there when I needed Him the most. It took several months before I realized that I was the problem. I had let my sorrows consume me. God hadn't moved. I'd moved.

When I came to my senses, I felt a deep joy in knowing that nothing was going to separate me from God. I was not going to give up on Him, and He was not going to give up on me. I will always need His wisdom, guidance, and love, and He will always be ready, able, and willing to help me overcome my doubts and fears.

Hardships in life prove or disprove our faith. Genuine believers don't base their faith on God fixing all their problems. They base their faith on the character of God. Like David in Psalm 13, they confidently proclaim: "I have trusted in your faithful love" (Ps. 13:5).

For Further Thought

When you feel lonely or forgotten, I encourage you to read Psalm 139:7–12 and Romans 8:35–39. They will remind you that you are never forgotten or alone.

Don't Avoid Maturity

There are reasons to set up rules of engagement in families when dealing with physical abuse, sexual abuse, drug abuse, and criminal behavior. But apart from those sensitive situations, I'm concerned about teachings that encourage Christians to set up boundaries and isolate themselves from family members who are simply difficult or annoying.

Scripture doesn't tell us to judge which of our family members are worthy of our time and effort and which are not. Instead of avoiding difficult relationships, the Bible instructs us to deal with problems constructively, openly, and considerately.

Reconciliation can be a messy process because it forces us to work through misunderstandings and honestly evaluate our own attitudes and actions. We do it because working through problems is important (Ps. 34:14; Prov. 10:12; Prov. 17:9, 17). Nowhere are we told to isolate ourselves from difficulty. In fact, if we avoid difficult family members, we usually end up becoming one.

> One who isolates himself pursues selfish desires;
> he rebels against all sound judgment. (Prov. 18:1)[1]

It's easy to get along with people we enjoy, but our faith is tested and refined by people whose behavior challenges us to grow in our relationship skills. If it weren't for these people, we'd never learn how to return good for evil and deny ourselves in a Christlike way (Rom. 12:9–21). This doesn't mean we accept abuse. It means we pursue peace.

For Further Thought

How can Matthew 5:9 and Luke 6:35 offer comfort when you are dealing with difficult people and difficult situations?

---

1. Some translations use the word *unfriendly* in Proverbs 18:1, but the Hebrew word means to separate or isolate.

Sacred Songs

The psalms are sacred poems and songs, so it's no surprise that they repeatedly encourage us to sing.

> Sing about the glory of his name; make his praise glorious. (Ps. 66:2)

> Sing for joy to God our strength; shout in triumph to the God of Jacob. (Ps. 81:1)

> Sing a new song to the LORD; let the whole earth sing to the LORD. (Ps. 96:1)

> Sing to him, sing praise to him; tell about all his wondrous works! (Ps. 105:2)

God created singing and music as a powerful influence in our lives. It's one of many ways we can express our emotions biblically and bring glory to His name. Music can change our mood, inspire us to action, and bring us to tears. It can soothe and calm us or make us angry and arrogant. It can focus our thoughts on the Lord or on immorality and worldliness.

When we sing, God isn't concerned with the quality of our singing voice. I like how the KJV translates Psalm 100:1 as "Make a joyful noise." But God is concerned with the influences in our lives, and music is a powerful influence. This doesn't mean all of our music must have a Christian theme, but it should at least be healthy for our spirits.

I encourage you to include uplifting Christian music in your daily schedule. It is especially important when dealing with discouragement.

For Further Thought

You might enjoy doing a word study of *sing* in the Psalms. Every time *sing* is used, note the context. It will give you a fuller idea of the beauty and purpose of singing to the Lord.

Five Keys to Trusting God Wholeheartedly

Most Christians know Proverbs 3:5a by heart: "Trust in the LORD with all your heart." It's a powerful, succinct truth—easy to memorize and recite but not always easy to live. That's one reason it's important to study the context of the verse to gain insights on trusting God with our whole heart. The following are five aspects mentioned in Proverbs 3:5-12, but I encourage you to study the whole chapter for additional insights.

1. *Don't "rely on" (trust) human understanding (v. 5).* Have you ever spent the whole day thinking through a problem before realizing you'd never prayed about it? I have, and it's genuinely a waste of time.

2. *Acknowledge God in everything we do, speak, and think (v. 6).* This always changes our perspective and purpose.

3. *Don't think too highly of ourselves. Realize our desperate need for God (v. 7).* The world encourages us to affirm and esteem ourselves. Scripture teaches us to affirm and esteem God.

4. *Prove our trust for God by honoring Him with more than mere words (v. 9).* If we're talking the talk, we need to be walking the walk.

5. *Accept God's loving rebuke and discipline (vv. 11–12).* God rebukes and disciplines us because He loves us (Heb. 12:1–11; Rev. 3:19).

When we trust God, He doesn't promise us smooth paths, but He promises us something better: godly paths (v. 6).

For Further Thought

What other insights can you gain from this passage?

Trust in the LORD with all your heart, and do not rely on your own understanding; in all your ways know him, and he will make your paths straight. Don't be wise in your own eyes; fear the LORD and turn away from evil. This will be healing for your body and strengthening for your bones. Honor the LORD with your possessions and with the first produce of your entire harvest; then your barns will be completely filled, and your vats will overflow with new wine. Do not despise the LORD's instruction, my son, and do not loathe his discipline; for the LORD disciplines the one he loves, just as a father disciplines the son in whom he delights. (Prov. 3:5–12)

I'm Not Listening

I was sitting in a coffee shop, studying Psalm 66, trying to grasp the meaning of verse 18: "If I had been aware of malice [sin, iniquity, wickedness] in my heart, the Lord would not have listened."

How can an omniscient, omnipresent God stop listening?

Just then, a mother and her small daughter sat down at the table next to mine. You could tell they loved each other as the little girl climbed into her mother's lap and began eating a large muffin.

"Don't take such big bites," her mother warned. "You'll make yourself sick."

The child glanced at her mom defiantly and stuffed the rest of the muffin into her small mouth.

"Time out," her mom said, moving her from her lap to the chair across from her. "You didn't listen to me. You need to think about what you've done." With a mouth full of muffin, the child began protesting. "I'm not listening," her mother said calmly.

Aha! I thought. That's the meaning of verse 18. When we defy God, He puts us in a type of "time out" so we can consider what we've done and repent. He still loves us, but He stops "listening" to our excuses until we are ready to give up our rebellion and climb back into His lap.

The psalmist understood the importance of confession, and that's why he proclaimed, "God has listened; he has paid attention to the sound of my prayer. Blessed be God! He has not turned away my prayer or turned his faithful love from me" (vv. 19–20).

For Further Thought

How do 1 John 1:8–10; John 9:31; and James 4:3 reinforce this truth in Psalm 66:18?

Anger Management

All of us have feelings of anger from time to time, and Proverbs offers excellent insights for dealing with those feelings.

1. *Patience shows maturity; anger shows immaturity.* We need to deal deliberately with anger if we want to mature in the Lord.

> A patient person shows great understanding, but a quick-tempered one promotes foolishness. (Prov. 14:29)

2. *Self-control involves careful use of words.* When discussing differences, wise Christians stick to the subject. They don't attack or discredit those who disagree with them. They use gracious words and avoid sarcasm and mockery.

> A gentle answer turns away anger, but a harsh word stirs up wrath. (Prov. 15:1)

3. *Self-control is more important than skill and power.* Anger can define us, making our good qualities seem insignificant.

> Patience is better than power, and controlling one's emotions, than capturing a city. (Prov. 16:32)

4. *Sometimes we can avoid anger by overlooking unimportant offenses.* Not everything needs to be addressed in a relationship. Some things should simply be forgiven.

> A person's insight gives him patience, and his virtue is to overlook an offense. (Prov. 19:11)

5. *We improve our self-control by choosing mature companions.* People influence us for good or bad.

> Don't make friends with an angry person, and don't be a companion of a hot-tempered one, or you will learn his ways and entangle yourself in a snare. (Prov. 22:24–25)

Most of us could use more patience and self-control, and memorizing, reciting, and pondering verses like these can be helpful. God's Word has a powerful effect on our lives and our habits.

For Further Thought

Psalm 37:8 is a good verse to memorize and recite when dealing with angry feelings. What other verses in this devotion might be helpful for that purpose?

Lifetime Students of Scripture

I recently listened to a teacher who used multiple Scripture references to support his political opinions. Sadly, the Bible passages didn't actually mean what he claimed they meant. Proverbs 18:2 describes this problem: "A fool does not delight in understanding, but only wants to show off his opinions."

It's bad enough when people share foolish viewpoints but even more serious when they misuse Scripture to do it. That's why it's absolutely essential that we study Scripture on our own and understand what it teaches, storing up accurate knowledge (Prov. 10:14).

Proverbs 9:9 says, "Instruct the wise, and he will be wiser still; teach the righteous, and he will learn more." We must be lifetime students of God's Word, always learning and gaining insights and discernment that will protect us from false teaching and foolish choices in life.

Psalm 119:29-32 expresses the passion we should all have for God's Word: "Keep me from the way of deceit and graciously give me your instruction. I have chosen the way of truth; I have set your ordinances before me. I cling to your decrees; LORD, do not put me to shame. I pursue the way of your commands, for you broaden my understanding."

The psalmist understood his great need for God's instruction, knowing it alone would keep him from deception and shame. May God give us that same passion.

For Further Thought

Psalm 119:9–16 is another passage that explains how God's Word keeps us on the right path in life. What insights can you glean from these verses?

Open Wide Your Mouth

When you first read Psalm 81:10, it might not make sense: "Open your mouth wide, and I will fill it." It's a poetic way to explain God's desire to nourish, satisfy, and bless us spiritually.

Sadly, our disobedience can prevent us from enjoying spiritual blessings. The promised land was described as "flowing with milk and honey." If God's people had not been so stubborn, He'd have fed them with the finest of wheat and satisfied them "with honey from the rock" (Ps. 81:11-16).

But God didn't offer the Israelites the promised land to simply make them wealthy landowners or give them good food to eat. His ultimate goal was to make them a nation of godly people so they could eventually share God's truths with the pagan nations around them. God's first priority is always the spiritual well-being of His people. He gives and withholds with that purpose in mind.

When Psalm 81:10 says, "Open your mouth wide, and I will fill it," it makes me think of baby birds, hungrily opening their mouths so they can be fed. They are totally dependent on their parents and know they cannot feed themselves. We need to have that same understanding of our need for spiritual food from the Lord.

We should hunger for God's guidance and wisdom and thirst for His righteousness. When we seek God with fervor and single-mindedness, He promises to feed our hungry spirits (Jer. 29:13).

So open your mouth wide, and He will fill it with food for your soul.

For Further Thought

A number of passages speak of God's feeding us spiritually. For example, Psalm 36:7–8; Matthew 4:4; and 5:6.

Magnify the Lord with Me

S cripture helps us examine our attitudes. For example, when we read Psalm 34:3, we should ask ourselves "What am I magnifying today?"

> O magnify the LORD with me, and let us exalt his name together. (Psalm 34:3 KJV)

Sometimes I dwell on sad situations I can't fix, health problems that cause me discomfort, or annoying interruptions in my schedule. But when I read Psalm 34:3, it convicts me to quit magnifying my problems and start magnifying the Lord.

Magnifying the Lord doesn't mean we can add to His greatness. We can't. He is already infinitely wise, wonderful, loving, just, pure, and holy. We run out of superlatives when we try to describe Him adequately. Magnifying the Lord means acknowledging, celebrating, and proclaiming His wonderful character.

When problems seem to overwhelm us, we can magnify the Lord by remembering that no one who puts hope in the Lord will ever be put to shame (Ps. 25:3). We can celebrate the fact that He will never leave us. He is "a helper who is always found in times of trouble" (Ps. 46:1). We can proclaim that He will sustain us and keep us from being shaken in any circumstance (Ps. 55:22).

As a child of the King, we have access to His infinite wisdom, strength, power, love, and knowledge! Magnifying the Lord helps us regain our perspective. His greatness makes our biggest problems seem small and insignificant.

So "magnify the LORD with me, and let us exalt his name together!"

For Further Thought

How might you magnify (acknowledge, celebrate, or proclaim) God's glory today? Some suggestions: share something about God's goodness with a friend, go on a prayer walk praising God for the beauty He has built into creation, or start a new habit of reading a psalm of praise before supper.

Flea Market Integrity

As a writer, I love old typewriters. So when I saw one at a flea market in Europe, I was excited. But while I was trying to decide if I could get it home in my suitcase, the seller doubled the price.

Flea markets give us an interesting glimpse into the local culture, revealing what people treasure. But some things are universal: in every nation and at every flea market, we find generous and honest people as well as greedy and dishonest people.

Proverbs 20:14 describes a common bargaining tactic: "'It's worthless, it's worthless!' the buyer says, but after he is on his way, he gloats." I've never used this tactic, but there were a few times I subdued my excitement at finding something I liked because I didn't want the seller to raise the price as the woman did with the typewriter.

Yes, flea markets are one of many places in life we can observe people's integrity, and we can examine our integrity as well. I once bought an old Bible for a few dollars, and as I walked away, I discovered a ten-dollar bill tucked in the pages. The seller was surprised and grateful when I returned it. She gave me the Bible for free.

I've been walking with the Lord more than forty years, and I've learned that "better a little with righteousness than great income with injustice" (Prov. 16:8). How we live our lives reflects or denies our faith: "Whoever lives with integrity fears the LORD, but the one who is devious in his ways despises him" (Prov. 14:2).

For Further Thought

I think God was testing me when I found the ten-dollar bill in the Bible. I admit I had a fleeting thought about keeping it. After all, it was legally mine. But it made me think through not only the legality but the command in Matthew 7:12. See also Proverbs 11:24.

The Comfort of Knowing that God Is with Us

Psalm 46 begins with this wonderful assurance:

> God is our refuge and strength,
> an ever-present help in trouble.
> Therefore we will not fear, though the earth give way
> and the mountains fall into the heart of the sea,
> though its waters roar and foam
> and the mountains quake with their surging.
> (vv. 1–3 NIV)

And it concludes with this wonderful command:

> Be still, and know that I am God;
> I will be exalted among the nations,
> I will be exalted in the earth. (v. 10 NIV)

When I read this psalm, I think of a small child who wanders into a crowd and panics, thinking she's lost. From her perspective, it's as terrible as if the earth is trembling and the mountains are toppling into the sea. Tears stream down her face, and fear fills her heart until she looks up and realizes that her father has been at her side all the time. He's never left her. Lifting her into his arms, he says, "Be still. I'm here. I've had my eye on you the whole time. Nothing is going to separate us. I'm in charge."

When our problems seem huge and fear begins to set in, we need to do the same thing as this small child. We need to "look up" and climb into our Father's arms. He can "still" our souls, relieve our fears, and let us know that He's in charge.

For Further Thought

What insights into God's character are found in Psalm 68:5 and Psalm 103:13?

> God in his holy dwelling is
> a father of the fatherless
> and a champion of widows. (Ps. 68:5)

> As a father has compassion on his children,
> so the LORD has compassion on those who fear
> him. (Ps. 103:13)

Christians Speaking Up

Throughout human history men and women have tried to justify evil. There was a time when people thought up fantastic excuses to justify slavery in America. They even tried to use the Bible to support it.

Slaves had no voice, no rights, no way of standing up for themselves. We are grateful for those brave souls who spoke up to abolish slavery. Many of them were motivated by their faith in Christ.

We see a similar injustice in our present day. Unborn babies have no voice, no rights, no way of standing up for themselves. I'm grateful for the brave souls who are speaking up to abolish abortion. Most of them are also motivated by their faith in Christ.

Proverbs 24:11–12 seems especially pertinent:

> Rescue those being taken off to death,
> and save those stumbling toward slaughter.
> If you say, "But we didn't know about this,"
> won't he who weighs hearts consider it?
> Won't he who protects your life know?
> Won't he repay a person according to his work?

Christians know that God creates life in the womb (Ps. 139:13). We know we have a responsibility to "speak up for those who have no voice, for the justice of all who are dispossessed" (Prov. 31:8).

If I had lived during the days of slavery, I hope I would have been one of those who spoke up for my enslaved brothers and sisters. And I want to be remembered as someone who spoke up for my unborn brothers and sisters.

For Further Thought

How does God view children according to Psalm 127:3–5 and Psalm 128:3–4? How does our fallen culture view children?

The Apple of God's Eye

The phrase "apple of his eye" was used by Shakespeare in *A Midsummer Night's Dream*, but it is most famously known as a biblical term, a phrase found in several Old Testament passages. The CSB translates it less poetically and more accurately as "the pupil of his eye." Whether we use the phrase "apple of his eye" or "pupil of his eye," it means something we passionately cherish and protect.

In Psalm 17:8, David calls out to God: "Protect me as the pupil of your eye; hide me in the shadow of your wings." Deuteronomy 32:9–10 and Zechariah 2:8 tell us that God treats His people as the "pupil of his eye."

We instinctively protect and cherish our eyes, perhaps more than any other part of our bodies. Our eye's pupil is sensitive to the slightest touch, harmed by the tiniest particles, and critically important for our vision.

God cherishes His children as the apple of His eye. He is sensitive to our slightest needs and constantly aware of our concerns. Nothing happens to us without His full knowledge. How fitting if we respond to His great love by cherishing His instructions as the apple of our eye, refusing to let particles of sin obstruct our vision of right and wrong.

Keep my commands and you will live; guard my teachings as the apple of your eye. (Prov. 7:2 NIV)

For Further Thought

God provides a number of protections for the pupil: both the iris and cornea carefully protect the pupil from harmful light and particles. What a great illustration of His love and concern for us. Does this analogy help you better understand the way God cherishes and protects you?

Understanding the Curses in the Psalms

Have you ever wondered why some psalms contain curses against people and nations?

These imprecatory psalms[2] may sound cruel until we remember these three truths:

1. *The psalmists experienced vicious attacks on their families and countrymen.* Note this description in Psalm 10:8: "He waits in ambush near settlements; he kills the innocent in secret places. His eyes are on the lookout for the helpless."

The psalmists were very likely asking God to treat their enemies as their enemies had treated them, following the Old Testament law of an eye for an eye and a tooth for a tooth (Lev. 24:19–21).

2. *The psalmists were not talking about taking personal revenge. They were asking God to act.* "Oppose my opponents, LORD; fight those who fight me" (Ps. 35:1).

---

2. To *imprecate* means "to invoke a curse or call down evil on someone or something."

3. *They were offended for God's sake as well as their own.* "Remember how the enemy has mocked you, LORD, how foolish people have reviled your name" (Ps. 74:18 NIV).

The New Testament tells us to love our enemies and do good to those who persecute us (Matt. 5:43–48). We don't take revenge, but we agree with God's righteous anger for those who reject Him and do evil (John 3:36).

For Further Thought

Read Leviticus 24:19–21. This law was set in place to prevent people from enacting punishments harsher than the crime. Now read Matthew 5:38–40. How did Christ address that Old Testament law?

If a verse in an imprecatory psalm causes you concern, I encourage you to remember that God never fulfills ungodly requests. When we know the Lord, we understand Him as He is described in Jeremiah 9:23–24.

> This is what the Lord says:
> "The wise person should not boast in his wisdom;
> the strong should not boast in his strength;
> the wealthy should not boast in his wealth.
> But the one who boasts should boast in this:
> that he understands and knows me—
> that I am the Lord, showing faithful love,
> justice, and righteousness on the earth,
> for I delight in these things."
> This is the Lord's declaration.

Clean Stables

Christians should have no partnership with "Christian cults" who use the name of Jesus while denying or redefining essential doctrines of our faith such as the deity of Christ, the Trinity, the virgin birth, salvation by grace through faith, Christ as the only way of salvation, the concepts of heaven and hell, the moral laws, and the inerrancy of Scripture (2 Cor. 6:14–18).

Genuine Christian denominations agree on these essentials found in God's Word. However, they don't all agree on nonessential beliefs and practices. And many of these nonessential differences have been debated by Jesus-loving, Bible-believing Christians throughout church history.

So, how do we handle this? Should we let the nonessentials divide us? Proverbs 14:4 speaks to this situation in a unique way: "Where there are no oxen, the manger is clean; but much revenue *comes* by the strength of the ox" (Prov. 14:4 NASB, italic used in Scripture).

If I ended this devotion here, you might be scratching your head, but take a moment to think about the principle in this short verse. If we have no oxen, we can keep a clean, unproductive stable. But a productive stable is going to get messy.

The same is true with Christian fellowship. It can be a little messy to have fellowship with people outside our denomination, but unity in the body of Christ offers multiplied opportunities for ministry and growth, and it gives us opportunities to respect those who don't agree with our nonessential views.

So, what will you choose? A clean stable or a productive one?

For Further Thought

How does Colossians 3:12–14 reinforce this truth?

> Therefore, as God's chosen ones, holy and dearly loved, put on compassion, kindness, humility, gentleness, and patience, bearing with one another and forgiving one another if anyone has a grievance against another. Just as the Lord has forgiven you, so you are also to forgive. Above all, put on love, which is the perfect bond of unity.

The Proverbs 31 Wife

Most people are familiar with Proverbs 31, but I want to focus on verse 1, which is often overlooked: "The words of King Lemuel, a pronouncement that his mother taught him." This verse illustrates a powerful responsibility and a special privilege. King Lemuel's mother taught him the truths in this chapter. In turn, he taught them to his son, and God included them in His divinely inspired Word. This godly mother had a special role in God's kingdom.

I am always amazed that some people think the Bible somehow minimizes the importance of women. I believe it does the opposite. This chapter in Proverbs describes a godly wife, a skilled and industrious woman, a woman with brains and good sense. She's not only gracious and kind; she's an excellent household manager. And these characteristics can describe any woman, whether she's married or not.

> Strength and honor are her clothing. . . . Her mouth speaks wisdom, and loving instruction is on her tongue. . . . Her children rise up and call her blessed; her husband also praises her: "Many women have done noble deeds, but you surpass them all!" Charm

is deceptive and beauty is fleeting, but a woman
who fears the LORD will be praised. (vv. 25–26,
28–30)

I think Satan goes out of his way to deceive women into
thinking Scripture underestimates their worth, when it
actually highlights it. Wives don't have the same roles as
husbands because they aren't husbands, and husbands don't
have the same roles as wives because they aren't wives. But
Scripture clearly presents women as important, unique, and
relevant.

For Further Thought

Proverbs 31 is not a to-do list. Women don't need to make
and sell linen garments to be good wives. It's an example of
how one woman fulfilled her calling as a wife and mother.
How do Titus 2:3–5 and Acts 18:24–26 help develop the biblical role of wives? How do Romans 16:1–6, Galatians 3:28, and
Joel 2:28–29 confirm the importance of all women in God's
kingdom?

He Hears Every Word

Have you ever had someone accidentally dial your phone so you could hear them talking, but they didn't know you were there? Or have you ever had someone say "goodbye" on a phone call, thinking they had hung up? But instead of hanging up, their phone continued to record their conversation without their knowledge.

When this happens, the words they speak might be positive, or they might be offensive, comical, or shocking. After all, we don't share our true feelings with everyone, nor should we. There are times it's respectful to keep our thoughts and opinions to ourselves.

These situations are a good reminder that we never hide our true thoughts and feelings from our Lord. We might convince ourselves that it's right to do something dishonest, "but the LORD weighs hearts" (Prov. 21:2). We may do the right thing for the wrong reasons, "but the LORD weighs motives" (Prov. 16:2).

We don't need to accidentally dial God, and we can never "hang up" on Him. He not only hears every word we speak; He hears the words we don't speak. We may think we are getting away with something ungodly, but "a man's ways are before the Lord's eyes, and he considers all his paths" (Prov. 5:21).

So let's be aware of our Lord, give thought to our ways, and seek to please Him in all that we do (Prov. 4:26).

For Further Thought

Consider the words of Psalm 104:34 and Psalm 19:14, remembering that our thoughts affect our actions.

> May my meditation be pleasing to him;
> I will rejoice in the Lord. (Ps. 104:34)

> May the words of my mouth
> and the meditation of my heart
> be acceptable to you,
> Lord, my rock and my Redeemer. (Ps. 19:14)

Humble Gifts

David understood that God had specific purposes for his life. In Psalm 57:2, he says, "I call to God Most High, to God who fulfills his purpose for me." In Psalm 138:8, he says, "The LORD will fulfill his purpose for me."

Do you know that God has unique plans for your life as well? This truth is beautifully explained in Ephesians 2:10: "For we are his workmanship, created in Christ Jesus for good works, which God prepared ahead of time for us to do."

Sometimes Christians think their gifts are insignificant. They compare themselves with believers in public ministry. But God handpicked you and me for things that perfectly fit our skills, experiences, and opportunities. Most of us have humble gifts, but our faithfulness to God's purposes is every bit as important as those with large public ministries. We can rejoice that "a humble spirit will gain honor" (Prov. 29:23).

I love the stories in Scripture of humble, behind-the-scenes Christians. Tabitha is one of my favorites—the woman who changed her world by sewing clothes for widows (Acts 9:36–42). Then there's Andrew, who lived in the shadow of his older brother Simon Peter. But Andrew was the first disciple to believe in Christ, and he brought his brother Peter to Jesus (John 1:41).

God has purposes for you, and He will bless you as you humbly and faithfully fulfill your calling.

> A faithful person will have many blessings. (Prov. 28:20)

For Further Thought

Notice the impact of Tabitha's humble gifts and how God called special attention to her life, death, and resurrection in Scripture (Acts 9:36–42).

The Aroma of Coffee

I love the fragrance of freshly brewed coffee, and some experts believe the aroma of coffee may release powerful antioxidants in our body to protect nerve cells from stress-related damage even if we don't drink it.

Most of us understand the power of smells. A whiff of my mother's perfume always brings back sweet memories of her love. The scent of fresh baked bread can make me hungry even when I've just finished a meal. In contrast, the stench of burnt food can make me lose my appetite.

God created us multifaceted, and we are sensitive to things even when we aren't conscious of their influence. If something as simple as the aroma of coffee can improve our attitude and well-being, imagine how easily we can be affected by negative influences.

Proverbs 4:23 says, "Guard your heart above all else, for it is the source of life."

Television, movies, books, and music are powerful "aromas" in our lives. When they have violent, immoral, or worldly themes, they affect our attitudes and emotions even if we aren't aware they are doing so. These things can alter our "spiritual chemistry," soften our view of sin, and change our values without our realizing it.

Only as we breathe in the sweet "aroma" of God's Word can we guard our hearts. So let's regularly consider the influences in our lives and ask God to help us eliminate any that interfere with our faith.

For Further Thought

For you were once darkness, but now you are light in the Lord. Walk as children of light—for the fruit of the light consists of all goodness, righteousness, and truth—testing what is pleasing to the Lord. Don't participate in the fruitless works of darkness, but instead expose them. For it is shameful even to mention what is done by them in secret. Everything exposed by the light is made visible, for what makes everything visible is light. Therefore it is said: Get up, sleeper, and rise up from the dead, and Christ will shine on you. Pay careful attention, then, to how you walk—not as unwise people but as wise—making the most of the time, because the days are evil. So don't be foolish, but understand what the Lord's will is. (Eph. 5:8–17)

False Pride and False Blame

Perhaps the most misunderstood proverb is Proverb 22:6 (KJV): "Train up a child in the way he should go: and when he is old, he will not depart from it."

Forgetting that biblical proverbs are wise sayings and not promises, some people claim this proverb assures parents that if they do the right things, their children will be godly adults.

It's true that this proverb contains an important principle. How we raise our children has a huge impact on their lives. That's why Ephesians 6:4 commands us to nurture our children in the Lord. Parents will be held responsible by God for the way we raise our children. Furthermore, our actions, attitudes, and values can affect our children's behavior and lifestyles for generations to come.

But listen to this next statement carefully: parents are not ultimately responsible for their adult children's choices in life. Such a claim places a heavy burden of false guilt on godly parents whose children walk away from the Lord.

Ezekiel 18 talks about righteous men having evil sons and evil men having righteous sons, and it ends with this clear statement: "A son won't suffer punishment for the father's iniquity, and a father won't suffer punishment for the son's iniquity" (v. 20). If righteous men were promised righteous children, Ezekiel 18 wouldn't be in Scripture.

Sons and daughters can rebel against their parents' godly instruction and live ungodly lives. They can also rebel against their parents' ungodly instruction and live godly lives. Proverbs 22:6 contains an important principle, not a promise. Let's not misuse it.

For Further Thought

Read the story of Joash in 2 Chronicles 24 and Christ's warning in Matthew 10:34–39. How do these passages impact the statement in Proverbs 22:6? You might want to refer back to the Day 7 devotion which explains that not all Proverbs are promises.

When Babies Praise God

I feel privileged to have become a believer when I was pregnant with my daughter. God used many aspects of my pregnancy to teach me spiritual truths. When our daughter was born, I was keenly aware of God's miracle of new life, both physically and spiritually.

He taught me another truth through my baby daughter's habit of sweetly cooing while she slept. When she accompanied me to my weekly Bible study shortly after her birth, her coos were sweet background music to our prayers.

Psalm 8 begins with praise and says the most remarkable thing: "LORD, our LORD, how majestic is your name in all the earth! You have set your glory in the heavens. Through the praise of children and infants you have established a stronghold against your enemies, to silence the foe and the avenger" (vv. 1–2 NIV).

I am convinced that baby coos are a form of praise to our God.

After Christ cleansed the temple, the Pharisees were indignant because children were crying out to Him in praise. Jesus referred His critics to Psalm 8: "Have you never read:

You have prepared praise from the mouths of infants and nursing babies?" (Matt. 21:16).

Psalm 8 also says the praise of infants silences God's enemies. If the praises of babies can shut the mouth of Satan, let's do our part to do the same.

For Further Thought

Consider using your daily activities as praise prompts. For example, when you wash the dishes, praise God for His purity. When you drink a glass of water, thank Him for being living water to your thirsty soul. Think of activities that remind you of God's character so you will remember to praise Him throughout your day.

Our Willingness to Accept Correction

Our culture is convinced that our greatest need is praise. In fact, it's not popular to talk about correction, and don't mention rebuke unless you want to be rebuked. But wise Christians recognize our need for accountability.

Proverbs emphasizes correction. In fact, it teaches us that we can actually determine a person's wisdom and the quality of their faith based on their willingness to accept correction:

> Don't rebuke a mocker, or he will hate you; rebuke the wise, and he will love you. (Prov. 9:8)

> Instruct the wise, and he will be wiser still; teach the righteous, and he will learn more. (Prov. 9:9)

> Whoever loves discipline loves knowledge, but one who hates correction is stupid. (Prov. 12:1)

> A fool despises his father's discipline, but a person who accepts correction is sensible. (Prov. 15:5)

One who listens to life-giving rebukes will be at home among the wise. (Prov. 15:31)

A wise correction to a receptive ear is like a gold ring or an ornament of gold. (Prov. 25:12)

Notice this repeated truth: wise and godly people accept correction and learn from it. Fools hate correction and remain stubborn and stupid. It's a sign of maturing faith to listen to wise counsel, examine our attitudes and actions, and amend our ways. It helps us see our blind spots, helps us remain humble, keeps us honest, strengthens our faith, and increases our wisdom.

It's life changing!

For Further Thought

Read Exodus 18:13–24 and note how a man of enormous power and favor responded to advice from his father-in-law.

Let's Brag on God

Some of the most beautiful psalms are those that are fully devoted to bragging on God.

For example, Psalm 103 lists wonderful things God does for us highlighting His forgiveness, patience, and faithfulness. And it contains this loving description of His character in verse 13: "As a father has compassion on his children, so the LORD has compassion on those who fear him."

When was the last time you bragged about God's fatherly love and compassion?

Psalm 104 praises God as Creator and in verse 24 says, "How countless are your works, LORD! In wisdom you have made them all; the earth is full of your creatures."

When was the last time you bragged about the amazing design and wisdom in God's creation?

Psalms 105 begins with these words: "Give thanks to the LORD, call on his name; proclaim his deeds among the peoples." Following that theme, both Psalms 105 and 106 recount events in Israel's history and brag about specific deeds of God as He patiently, faithfully, and lovingly dealt with Israel despite her rebellion.

When was the last time you bragged about your personal history with God, remembering specific ways He has blessed you and your family?

Bragging on God is a great way to gain perspective, encourage a fellow believer, or share Christ with an unsaved friend. So let's do it today and every day.

For Further Thought

Sometimes the easiest way to witness to an unsaved neighbor or coworker is to talk about something God has done in our lives. I encourage you to pray for opportunities to do this, asking God to help you fit your "God stories" naturally into conversations.

A Daily Song

As a new believer, one of my favorite praise songs was Psalm 118:24: "This is the day the LORD has made; let's rejoice and be glad in it." I enjoyed singing this verse because it reminded me that every day God had purposes for my life (Eph. 2:10).

When the psalmist proclaimed, "This is the day," he was celebrating a particular victory, but we can use that phrase every day. In fact, Psalm 118:26 reminds us of that fact. It says, "He who comes in the name of the LORD is blessed," a phrase that was shouted when Christ made His triumphal entry (Matt.21:9). That makes me think of the triumphal entry Christ made into my heart and soul.

When I became a Christian, I began to understand that God is in charge of every minute, hour, and day of my life. That doesn't mean that every day goes exactly as we'd like it to go. It means that every day is an opportunity to live for the Lord and enjoy His love. And I cannot help but think of the wonderful day in our future called "the day of our Lord Jesus Christ" when He returns to take His people home (1 Cor. 1:8).

As believers we have reason to rejoice every day because the Lord is our strength and song, and He has become our salvation (Ps. 118:14). Every day we can rejoice in the refuge, comfort, and courage He gives us.

For Further Thought

Psalm 118:24 is an easy verse to memorize. Why not recite it every morning when you get out of bed?

If you read the two verses before verse 24, you'll find a beautiful prophecy of our Lord. Isaiah 28:16, Matthew 21:42, and Acts 4:10–11 will help you better understand this prophecy and why it should cause rejoicing.

The Proverbs 4 Walk

Have you noticed that most supermarkets put staples like milk and eggs at the back of the store? The owners know they'll sell more if people walk past aisles of tempting items they don't need. If we want to avoid those temptations, we can prepare a list beforehand. Then, when we get to the store, we can walk through the aisles keeping our eyes focused straight ahead, refusing to look to the right or the left. It's a great way to avoid overspending.

In our walk with the Lord, Satan uses methods similar to retail stores, hoping to distract us from God's purposes. He lines our path with temptations and opportunities for immorality, greed, drunkenness, thievery, selfishness, etc. Before we reach God's healthy, fulfilling goals, he wants to divert, delay, or derail us so we'll spend our lives on junk-food purposes.

The solution to this problem is found in Proverbs 4:25–27. It's what I call "the Proverbs 4 walk":

> Let your eyes look forward;
> fix your gaze straight ahead.
> Carefully consider the path for your feet,

and all your ways will be established.
Don't turn to the right or to the left;
keep your feet away from evil.

Let's prayerfully examine our priorities, making sure we are seeking to do those things God prepared in advance for us to do (Eph. 2:10).

For Further Thought

Are there ways you have been distracted from God's best by selfish or less important pursuits? How can you get back on the path?

The LORD makes firm the steps
of the one who delights in him;
though he may stumble, he will not fall,
for the LORD upholds him with his hand.
(Ps. 37:23–24 NIV)

Fools, Anger, Repentance

I'd rather not mention it, but Proverbs 28:13 says, "Whoever conceals their sins does not prosper, but the one who confesses and renounces them finds mercy" (NIV). So here goes: I sometimes lose my temper.

If you ask why I lose my temper, I'd like to tell you that it's when I'm tired or stressed or provoked, but that wouldn't be true. When we lose our temper, it's because we choose to sin. Or as Proverbs explains, it's because we're acting like fools: "Fools vent their anger" and "show their annoyance at once." In contrast, the wise quietly hold back their anger and overlook insults (Prov. 29:11 NLT; Prov. 12:16 NIV).

So, how should we respond when we lose our temper? This devotion would be of little value if I shared my foolish, sinful behavior without explaining how I deal with it.

When I lose my temper, I try to follow these three steps:

1. I repent and ask God's forgiveness (1 John 1:9).
2. I ask forgiveness of those whom I've offended (James 5:16).

3. I make it a matter of prayer and seek accountability if necessary, knowing that as I yield to God's Spirit, He will change me (Phil. 2:12–13).

Sensible people control their temper; they earn respect by overlooking wrongs. (Prov. 19:11 NLT)

I want to be a sensible person. How about you?

For Further Thought

Some people express their anger through silence, by giving people the silent treatment or the cold shoulder. These expressions of anger may be quieter, but they are still foolish and sinful.

Wise Counsel for Friendships

We should have non-Christian friends so we can share the love of Christ with them. But our closest relationships should be with godly Christians because "bad company corrupts good morals" and "a companion of fools will suffer harm" (1 Cor. 15:33; Prov. 13:20). This means we avoid close friendships with people who lack self-control (Prov. 25:28; 28:7), especially those who are hot-tempered or violent (Prov. 22:24–25; Prov. 16:29).

We also should choose friends based on their values, avoiding those who have worldly ethics, those who are financially dishonest (Prov. 1:10–19), or those who are impressed with money, prestige, and power (Prov. 19:4, 6–7). Likewise, we must avoid immoral and wicked people (Prov. 4:14–19).

On the flip side, "The one who walks with the wise will become wise" (Prov. 13:20). We want companions who encourage us when we need encouragement and correct us when we need correction (Prov. 27:6). This "sharpens" us, influencing us in positive ways (Prov. 27:17). We also want friends who forgive us and don't keep bringing up past offenses (Prov. 17:9). Those types of friends are willing to stand with us through good times and bad (Prov. 17:17).

These are the kinds of friends we want, and the first step in finding good friends is being one.

For Further Thought

Iron sharpens iron, and one person sharpens another. (Prov. 27:17)

How have godly relationships sharpened your social skills, moral values, and decision-making? If you don't have godly friendships, I encourage you to make it a matter of prayer.

When the Foundations Are Being Destroyed

Many of the psalms stress the sufficiency and importance of God's Word—His commands, instructions, laws, and wisdom. As our Creator, God alone has authority to define right and wrong. He alone knows what blesses and what damages us. The psalmists realized this and cherished God's Word as a protection for heart, mind, and soul.

In our present culture the foundations of truth and wisdom are being destroyed in three major ways (Ps. 11:3):

1. *Our culture is calling good evil and evil good (Isa. 5:20).* People take pride in perversion and they mock godliness (Ps. 12:7–8).

> Acquitting the guilty and condemning the just—
> both are detestable to the LORD. (Prov. 17:15)

2. *People believe they can do whatever they want without consequences.*

> In all his scheming, the wicked person arrogantly thinks, "There's no accountability, since there's no God." (Ps. 10:4)

3. *People exalt themselves.* People esteem and honor themselves instead of God, rejecting God's loving commands and trusting human wisdom.

> Do you see a person who is wise in his own eyes? There is more hope for a fool than for him. (Prov. 26:12)

We must have the same attitude toward God's Word the psalmists had:

> I delight in your commands, which I love. . . . The arrogant constantly ridicule me, but I do not turn away from your instruction. (Ps. 119:47, 51)

Do you believe God knows what is best for mankind? Are you prepared not only to live according to God's commands but also to speak up for them even if it brings you ridicule?

For Further Thought

Have you felt the pressure to deny unpopular commands in God's Word? Ask for God's help to stand firm.

> Therefore, my dear brothers and sisters, be steadfast, immovable, always excelling in the Lord's work, because you know that your labor in the Lord is not in vain. (1 Cor. 15:58)

The Saddest Psalm

Psalm 88 is the only psalm that has no resolution. The psalmist explains that he's like a dead man, cut off from God's care, in the lowest pit, overwhelmed with darkness. It's more a lament than a psalm, ending with this sad note: "Darkness is my only friend."

Many psalms start with this kind of discouragement or confusion, but they end with renewed hope in the Lord. Psalm 88 is different, unique among the psalms, because it ends as it begins with a hopeless outlook on life.

Job didn't write this psalm, but he cried out to God in similar fashion. Despite his strong faith, Job eventually found his pain and confusion overwhelming. In Job 3:11 he lamented, "Why was I not stillborn; why didn't I die as I came from the womb?" In Job 6:4, he accused, "Surely the arrows of the Almighty have pierced me."

God responded without explaining Job's sorrows. Instead, He reminded Job that He is God and Job is not: "You are God's critic, but do you have the answers?" (Job 40:2 NLT). This satisfied Job because, even though he'd lost hope, he never lost his faith. The same is true of the psalmist in Psalm 88. At his darkest hour, he cried out to God, not man, affirming God as "LORD, God of my salvation" (Ps. 88:1).

Even when we don't understand our circumstances, we can trust the character of God.

For Further Thought

How do Deuteronomy 29:29 and 1 Corinthians 13:12 give you comfort when you don't understand why bad things happen?

> The hidden things belong to the LORD our God, but the revealed things belong to us and our children forever, so that we may follow all the words of this law. (Deut. 29:29)

> For now we see only a reflection as in a mirror, but then face to face. Now I know in part, but then I will know fully, as I am fully known. (1 Cor. 13:12)

A Trusted Prescription

When I pick up a prescription at the pharmacy, I'm given several pages of detailed instructions for its use with warnings about the possible side effects. If I haven't used the medicine before, I read through these details and make sure it was correctly prescribed for my condition. But if I've used it before and I trust it, I don't bother.

When we trust something, it changes our perspective, and that's true when it comes to Scripture.

Sometimes I come across something in Scripture, typically in the Old Testament, and I don't understand it. That's when I "read the details": research the background, check into the original language, customs, and purpose of the passage. I also read what Bible scholars have written about the passage.

I do this extra research so I will know the answer if someone asks for clarification. I don't do it because I'm doubting God's Word. You see, I've been taking the "medicine" of God's Word for more than forty years with nothing but positive side effects (Ps. 1:1–3).

This extra research improves my knowledge, but I trust God's Word and His character regardless. That's because I daily benefit from the healing effects of Scripture. It consistently improves my spiritual well-being, protecting me from viral errors, chronic sins, and terminal hopelessness (Ps. 119:93).

I admit it. I'm addicted (Ps. 119:40). How about you? Are you taking a strong enough dosage of God's Word to keep your faith healthy?

For Further Thought

How does Psalm 119:25, 28, 92–93 affirm that God's Word is a healing "medicine" for our souls?

> My life is down in the dust;
> give me life through your word. (v. 25)

> I am weary from grief;
> strengthen me through your word. (v. 28)

> If your instruction had not been my delight,
> I would have died in my affliction.
> I will never forget your precepts,
> for you have given me life through them.
> (vv. 92–93)

Four Truths that Help Us Deal with Slander

A jealous coworker blames you for their mistake or takes credit for something you've done. An immature family member blows something out of proportion. A stubborn neighbor spreads a false rumor about you.

Most of us will be slandered, misunderstood, or maligned at some point in our lives. When David wrote Psalm 62, he was having this problem: "They take pleasure in lying; they bless with their mouths, but they curse inwardly" (v. 4).

Let's look at how David handled this difficult situation:

1. *He found comfort and peace in God alone.*
   I am at rest in God alone. (v. 1)

2. *He understood that God's judgment is what ultimately matters.*
   My salvation and glory depend on God, my strong rock. My refuge is in God. (v. 7)

3. *He recognized that God is always ready to listen to his problems.*

Trust in him at all times, you people; pour out
your hearts before him. God is our refuge. (v. 8)

4. *He knew that even though he may not see justice fully
played out here on earth, God will judge each person
correctly.*
For you repay each according to his works. (v. 12)

People may slander us and seem to get away with it. Bad
people will sometimes be honored, and good people will
sometimes be dishonored. But our God judges perfectly. He
rewards faithfulness and punishes sin. Even if everyone
turns against us, we can find our comfort and strength in
God alone.

For Further Thought

Matthew 5:11–12 and John 16:33 can also give us comfort
when we're slandered or misunderstood.

Our Words Reflect Our Heart

In Matthew 15:18, Jesus said, "What comes out of the mouth comes from the heart."

We may try to hide our anger, resentment, or pride, but eventually our words will give us away. However, if we deal biblically with bad attitudes and ungodly desires, our words will reflect that as well. This is especially important when we are sharing God's truth, advising a fellow Christian, or sharing our faith with an unbeliever.

Words can bless or curse, wound or heal, discourage or inspire, mislead or direct, soften or crush. Yes, "the heart of a wise person instructs his mouth" (Prov. 16:23).

I've had older Christian friends who've modeled healthy conversation patterns for me, showing discernment and wisdom. They've known what I needed to hear when I needed to hear it, whether correction or comfort (Prov. 15:23). They've chosen their words carefully and prayerfully, listening to me before responding (Prov. 10:32; 15:2, 28; 16:21). And they've known when to keep their mouths shut (Prov. 10:19). Their hearts were reflected in their words, and that made their words valuable to me (Prov. 10:20–21).

I want my heart to reflect that same wisdom and grace, so I join David in praying, "May the words of my mouth and the meditation of my heart be acceptable to you, LORD, my rock and my Redeemer" (Ps. 19:14).

Would you like to join me in that prayer?

For Further Thought

I encourage you to look up each verse referenced in this devotion and consider memorizing those that would help you develop wise and godly speech. And let me add an additional one from the New Testament: "My dear brothers and sisters, understand this: Everyone should be quick to listen, slow to speak, and slow to anger" (James 1:19).

Wisdom from Psalm 16

Have you ever pursued a goal you thought would make you happy only to find out it didn't live up to your expectations? Did you know that puts you in the same category as the wisest man on earth?

Solomon's wisdom was greater than the other wise men of his day, yet he wasted most of his life on extravagant wealth, pleasure, women, and worldly honor (1 Kings 4:30; 11). Only later in life when he looked back at all he'd achieved did he say, "Everything was meaningless, a chasing after the wind; nothing was gained under the sun" (Eccles. 2:11 NIV).

Solomon's father David also wasted his time on some empty pursuits, but whenever he got off track, he'd repent and remember this truth, which he wrote in Psalm 16: "You are my Lord; I have nothing good besides you" (v. 2). He understood that the Lord was his greatest treasure, and anything good in his life he credited to the Lord: "LORD, you are my portion and my cup of blessing; you hold my future" (Ps. 16:5).

Our relationship with God is more valuable than anything the world has to offer. No matter what circumstances affect our lives here on earth, we know that He is at our right hand and we won't be shaken (Ps. 16:8). Best of all, we will enjoy His presence throughout eternity (Ps. 16:10–11).

Do you understand that apart from the Lord you have no good thing?

For Further Thought

How do Matthew 6:19–20 and 1 Timothy 6:17–19 confirm the truth in Proverbs 23:4–5?

> Do not wear yourself out to get rich;
> do not trust your own cleverness.
> Cast but a glance at riches, and they are gone,
> for they will surely sprout wings
> and fly off to the sky like an eagle.
> (Prov. 23:4–5 NIV)

A Multitude of Counselors

When Proverbs 15:22 tells us to seek "many advisers," it doesn't mean we should keep looking until we find a counselor who gives the advice we want to hear.

Approval is always more appealing than correction, and we'll have no trouble finding teachers and counselors who will give us selfish advice (Prov. 12:15; Prov. 14:16). Advisors who help people fulfill selfish agendas will always be more popular than those who suggest self-sacrifice, self-denial, and godly goals.

If we let our fallen human nature reign, we'll seek out counselors who encourage us to ignore God's commands and blame shift our problems onto others. We'll seek out career counselors who tell us to focus on happiness, not holiness. And we'll listen to the people who tell us we can compromise God's values.

But Proverbs 15:22 isn't telling us to seek out worldly counselors. It's telling us to seek out wise, experienced, and God-fearing counselors who will not be afraid to correct us when we are wrong (Prov. 9:10).

It's wonderful to have approval and acceptance, but Christians understand that we sometimes need rebuke and correction. When Proverbs 27:6 says, "The wounds of a friend are trustworthy," it's encouraging us to accept valid correction from people who care enough about us to correct us with principles from God's Word.

So, whenever we are facing decisions, let's pray, carefully consider our options, and seek multiple godly advisors.

For Further Thought

How does 2 Timothy 4:3 add insights to this devotion?

> For the time will come when people will not tolerate sound doctrine, but according to their own desires, will multiply teachers for themselves because they have an itch to hear what they want to hear.

Aware of Our Surroundings

We were in a small European café when two men came in and sat at the table next to ours. They acted as if they were waiting for someone, but they slowly began edging their chairs closer to us.

Just then our waiter came to our table, bent down and whispered, "Please watch your purse and backpack. These men are acting suspiciously." Within moments the two men disappeared, aware we'd recognized their purpose. I was grateful for our waiter's warning to be aware of our surroundings. And it's a good warning for our spiritual lives as well.

John 10:10 tells us that there is "a thief [who] comes only to steal and kill and destroy" us spiritually. He is always on the prowl. Instead of guarding our backpacks and purses, we need to be guarding our hearts. We must carefully choose our music, reading materials, internet influences, entertainment, and companions. Satan will use any ungodly influence to steal our peace, wisdom, and devotion to God.

Proverbs 4:23 poetically warns us of this danger: "Guard your heart above all else, for it is the source of life." If we are going to protect ourselves from the thief, we need to keep our minds focused on the Lord (Prov. 23:19).

Are you aware of your spiritual surroundings? Are there influences in your life that are distracting you from God's purposes?

> There are thorns and snares on the way of the crooked; the one who guards himself stays far from them. (Prov. 22:5)

For Further Thought

Have you made the same decision the psalmist makes in Psalm 101:3 (AMP)? "I will set no worthless or wicked thing before my eyes. I hate the practice of those who fall away [from the right path]; it will not grasp hold of me."

The Beginning, Not the End

When we recite Proverbs 9:10, "The fear of the LORD is the beginning of wisdom," *fear* is probably the most difficult word to understand. But I think the most overlooked and underestimated word in the verse is *beginning*.[3]

Let me explain. When we fear the Lord, we begin to realize His infinite wisdom, love, glory, and perfection. We realize our need to know Him better and become familiar with His Word and His ways.

So, why do I think we overlook the word "beginning"? Because fearing the Lord is the *beginning* of our walk with God, not the end, but we Christians are notorious for "sitting down" in our salvation instead of moving forward into maturity. We plan our finances, our career, our families, and even our meals for the week, but we rarely plan our growth in Christ.

Wisdom isn't something that just happens to us. It's something we seek: "Wisdom is supreme—so get wisdom. And whatever else you get, get understanding" (Prov. 4:7).

---

3. The biblical meaning of fear is described in the devotion for Day 8.

Proverbs 23:23 says, "Buy—and do not sell—truth, wisdom, instruction, and understanding." This doesn't mean we buy it in the literal sense although that may be the case when we pay for Christian materials or training classes. But it means we spend effort and time to understand God's will (Rom. 12:1–2).

Let's not stop at the beginning.

For Further Thought

Take time today to make at least one plan that will improve your knowledge, wisdom, and understanding of our Lord.

> Give thanks to the LORD, call on his name;
> proclaim his deeds among the peoples.
> Sing to him, sing praise to him;
> tell about all his wondrous works!
> Boast in his holy name;
> let the hearts of those who seek the Lord rejoice.
> Seek the LORD and his strength;
> seek his face always. (Ps. 105:1–4)

Using *Wisdom for Life*
for Small-Group Study

Although *Wisdom for Life* is designed for individual devotional use, the "For Further Thought" sections and the referenced Scripture passages make it ideal for family devotions or small-group study as well.

If using it for a small group, choose several devotions to discuss each week, depending on the amount of time you have for the study. You can choose them in the order of the book or choose them with a particular theme, as suggested on the following pages.

You can read the chosen devotions together, read all referenced Scripture passages, and discuss the "For Further Thought" sections. In addition, you can encourage group members to read one psalm and/or one chapter of Proverbs each day while taking the study. Then, if time allows, they can share insights they've learned from their personal reading during the week.

On the following pages you'll find suggested collections according to theme.

Understanding Psalms

Goal: To gain an overview of the beauty and relevance of the book of Psalms.

Day 2—Prophecy, Principles, Praise, and Problem-Solving
Day 3—Old Letters in the Attic
Day 4—The Relevance of the Psalms
Day 5—Figurative and Poetic Language
Day 9—Good Prayers from Psalms
Day 15—Precious Predictions of Christ
Day 67—Sacred Songs
Day 78—Understanding the Curses in the Psalms

Understanding Proverbs

Goal: To introduce the practical wisdom and unique features of the book of Proverbs.

Day 5—Figurative and Poetic Language
Day 6—A Proverb a Day Keeps Stupidity Away
Day 7—The Difference between a Proverb and a Promise
Day 8—The Beginning of Wisdom
Day 100—The Beginning, Not the End

Misunderstandings

Goal: To address subjects and Scripture passages that are easily misunderstood.

Day 18—Do We Become What We Think?
Day 19—The Main Priority
Day 26—Glory to God, Not Man
Day 29—Why Would We Hide It?
Day 30—Whose Heart Are You Going to Trust?

Day 37—A Foolish Contradiction?
Day 45—The Desires of God's Heart
Day 54—What about Promises for Health and Protection?
Day 61—Unanswered Prayer
Day 69—I'm Not Listening
Day 93—The Saddest Psalm
Day 84—False Pride and False Blame

Acting Wisely

Goal: To address a variety of behaviors such as honesty and wholesome speech.
Day 33—Biblical "Rules of Speech"
Day 36—Bruised Berries
Day 46—Self-Esteem or Self-Control?
Day 57—Fake News and Faulty Sources
Day 60—Warnings against Sexual Sins
Day 70—Anger Management
Day 74—Flea Market Integrity
Day 79—Clean Stables
Day 81—He Hears Every Word
Day 86—Our Willingness to Accept Correction
Day 96—Our Words Reflect Our Heart

Seeking Healthy Relationships

Goal: To address issues that make or break relationships.
Day 49—Pure in Our Own Eyes
Day 50—Exaggeration or Aggressive Pursuit?
Day 66—Don't Avoid Maturity
Day 90—Fools, Anger, Repentance
Day 91—Wise Counsel for Friendships

Overcoming Discouragement and Adversity

Goal: To encourage those who are discouraged or those facing challenges and difficulties.

God's Life-Changing Word

Goal: To show the relevance and importance of spending time regularly in God's Word.

Day 29—Why Would We Hide It?
Day 53—Wisdom, Joy, and Radiance in Psalm 19
Day 63—Three Powerful Truths in the Shortest Psalm
Day 71—Lifetime Students of Scripture
Day 94—A Trusted Prescription
Day 100—The Beginning, Not the End

Three Essential Ingredients in Christian Faith

Goal: To reinforce our need for prayer, praise, and repentance.
Day 19—The Main Priority
Day 31—The Refreshment of Repentance
Day 32—Don't Trivialize God's Name!
Day 48—Listening When We Pray
Day 51—If You Have Breath
Day 73—Magnify the Lord with Me
Day 87—Let's Brag on God
Day 90—Fools, Anger, Repentance

Standing Firm

Goal: To encourage unwavering faith despite the challenges of our anti-Christian culture.
Day 27—Standing Firm in Our Anti-Christian Culture
Day 34—The Commands of a Loving Father
Day 38—Psalm 12 for Today
Day 41—"Judge-Not" Confusion
Day 42—Will You Conform?
Day 58—They Think God Is Just Like Them
Day 62—What Chains?
Day 64—What's in a Name?
Day 76—Christians Speaking Up

Inspiration to Persevere

Goal: To reinforce our need to remain strong in all circumstances.

Of Special Interest to Women

Goal: To highlight issues of specific interest to women.

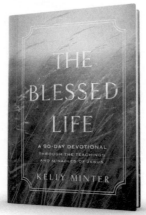

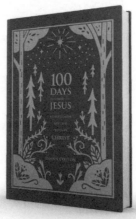